The Lover's Man-ual

The Lover's

Man-ual

Dedicated to Lateacha A. Coleman. I hate you aren't here to see the finished product. But your courage pushed me forward to finish. I will make you proud. I will always love you. Your brother.

N.M. Porterfield

Acknowledgements

I would like to first thank the love of my life Amexia Harris (soon to be Porterfield), for showing me that love really does exist. You are my gift from God, I am forever grateful for your presence in my life. To my firstborn son Jeremiah, thank you for giving me new life and the strength and motivation to push through when I thought I was at the end of my rope. I love you and hope that the love I show you will be lesson enough to give you guidance for your life. Thank you to the family members and friends who were with me during this book project. Your patience and support was invaluable. To all of the women who I had become involved with in the past, I thank you for the lesson you brought into my life. I hope that everyone can take something from my life experiences and the lessons in love that I've amassed over my years of romantic escapades. Remember that you are responsible for the Lover you become. All I can do is give you the guide. Thank you the reader for purchasing this book. It's for you that I embarked on this journey in the first place. Enjoy.

<u>Introduction</u>

Love-an emotion that is generally characterized by a strong bond between two individuals. A term that floats between perfection and disaster depending on the person or people involved, and like a fool I intended to be its master. I was a ladies man, a man who loved women, an appreciator of the female species, the ultimate Lover's man. Everything about them enticed me, pulled me in. I had to know what they liked, what they loved, what they hated and why. In some weird way I wanted every woman in the world to love me, and in return to be loved by them. Thus began my ego trip which added more than a few stamps on my passport. But Love, like most things, doesn't always pan out the way we hope.

I originally was going to do a book about all of my sexual exploits. A tell-all of sorts. Just a book bragging and boasting about my conquests in the bedroom. But as erotic as it could have been, it would have lacked substance and I believe there is more to those experiences than just mindless sex. Through my maturation I had discovered certain methods that gave me more control over my relationships and the direction they took. What began as a trial and error method of dating became a code that was formulated from my many, many experiences.

I entered into dating knowing exactly what I wanted, and when and how I would get it. The ball remained in my court. Whether I wanted a sexual fix or someone meaningful, I could maximize my gain and minimize the risks I took in dating. No longer was I playing a guessing game with women trying to figure out what I had to say or do to get things accomplished. I knew exactly how to get what I wanted.

Evolution. It's about becoming something greater than you were. Rewriting your own design to incorporate something more into your way of life. The strong dominate. The weak are weeded out and love is no different. We evolve, or we die out. I am an apex predator, though I didn't start off that way. Growing pains, loss, heartache, more than anything persistence helped me become the lover that I am today.

So what's the difference? What's the difference between me and you? How am I able to deal with relationships successfully while most people struggle figuring out if they're going to get a call back or not? What sets me apart?

Four things: Intelligence, charisma, adaptability, and follow-through. These are the four characteristics that define the perfect lover. Man or woman, if you have these characteristics you will be a diamond amongst coals. Evolution. Growth. Change. If you do not, you're destined to repeat the same catastrophic results that you've experienced in relationships before. Commit yourself to a new way of thinking. A new methodology to relationships. Approach romance with a new mindset. Make love your bitch. It's time to shed the old skin and become someone new.

When I speak of intelligence it is not a reference to your actual IQ. Instead you must be of a curious nature with a desire to learn and comprehend the concepts that will make you better. There is a lot to be learned in this world of love. Learned from yourself, learned from your past, and learned from the person that you are currently dealing with. These lessons should NOT be taken lightly. Instead they should be inscribed upon your heart and used as the tools to constantly improve upon your own understanding. If you ever stop thirsting for the knowledge to make yourself better, then you have ultimately given rise to your own demise.

Charisma is nothing more than the ability to get people to like you and to get them to do the things you want them to do. Charismatic people tend to be leaders but you can use this trait to be something else. Something sexy, sensual, appealing to more than just yourself. Love is all about relationships. Relationships are about relating. If you cannot connect, you cannot implement anything you learn about love and seduction. Make people like you, this will open the door so that your intellect can shine through.

Adaptability means shaping yourself to your environment. Adjusting to different people, different places, different circumstances and evolving into something that is more dominant. Do not let your circumstances control you. Do not let your relationships control you. You control them. Make the change necessary to be successful and you will be successful.

Persistence is necessary. Even when making a change you must continue the change for it to become a habit. Beyond that, you must continue further for it to become a behavior. We don't want temporary successes and short term victories. We want continual success in love, in relationships, in sex, in all areas of romance. This doesn't come from trying it one day and seeing it doesn't work. You have to stick with it. Everything I say to you I have found to be true. I put my life, my love, my mistakes, and successes into a form that you can learn from. I hope that it takes you far.

The Lovers Man-ual is a book about the rules of effective dating and the pitfalls you should avoid when engaging romantically with another individual. Finding love was something that I myself desired so much. Yet in my journey to discover loves secrets I saw mostly lies, pain, and disappointment. They say experience is the best teacher. Well when it comes to love and women I should have a PhD. I can't say my way was perfect, it's actually far from it. I made a lot of mistakes and had to learn from them the hard way. What I can leave is my Man-ual. A man's

perspective on accounts of love, self-identity,and evolution into

manhood. I have romanced women from all walks of life.

Women who came from different backgrounds,races and creeds.

I've changed my definition of love more times than I've changed

addresses. My experiences changed my perception of not just

love, but of myself, and the world we live in. Follow me as I

recount my life in a few short chapters of drama, passion, hate,

and love and discover the lover inside of you. This is my

manifesto. This is the Lover's Man-ual

1

<u>History's Lesson</u>

What does the past tell us? As we dive into our world of love the first thing we want to do is forget the past and move on. That's wrong. Everything has a beginning, even love. But how you love does not start with just you. How you perceive it, process it, and receive it are all factors determined by you, but they don't start with you.

For that you have to take a trip back. All the way back to your childhood. Back to when your parents were dating. When *their* parents were dating. All of this is indicative of how you will play games of the heart. Love is an interesting thing. It comes to us in many forms. Everyone's definition of it is different. So in order to understand how you love, we have to rewind to a time before you yourself knew love.

Pre-history-In the beginning there were mistakes. Mistakes heartbreaks and wasted time, money and emotion, but this is natural for a lot of relationships. Nobody starts off with all the answers. Even if they have them, most people won't adhere to the teachings passed down from those who did it before them.

Hard-headed does not begin to describe the average lover. We watch movies and listen to songs and think we've got it all. The beginning always seems like it's the roughest. But it's the years after that are actually the hardest and the most instrumental in shaping your *love identity* . Relationships, sex, break-ups, arguments, first times, last days and more all lay in our wake, but first we have to start with a beginning. Most people believe that their dating habits started with the first person they dated but in reality it started long before. Who you are dictates how you date. To become the best lover you can be you must first learn who you are.

I came from a family with no dad in the home. He was a part of my life, but was disconnected in a way because I didn't live with him. He was a good man, but as my father I felt the weight of his absence more than his presence. This made a difference. As I became the man I am today and think back on the types of women I dated, my habits and characteristics were all factors influenced, positively and/or negatively, by my parents. This is usually the case in instances where there are two parents present in the home. With opposite sex single caregivers, the individual usually struggles with understanding their role. With same sex single caregivers, the individual struggles understanding the opposite sex. In cases where the same sex parent is the only one available, we learn from what we see that parent do in regards to the opposite sex. This is also a positively or negatively affected thought process. If your mom seemed like someone you could be with forever you would look for someone like her. If you hated your mom you will look for someone who was the opposite. A woman can tell you all about a woman's wants and needs but can never tell you how to be a man. In the same sense, a man can tell you what a guy desires but can't give you a play-by-play on womanhood. This is not because of the superiority of one sex over the other, but because women and men are physiologically and emotionally and mentally different. So for those single parents, try to introduce your children to positive role models of the same and opposite sex in order to give them proper exposure to love and life.

Parents are the starting point. There is a lot you can learn from mom and dad about why you love the way you do. This is the foundational point that aims the arrow. Once that arrow is fired it tends to stay on the same path, meaning that whatever dating methods you start with, you usually maintain these habits long into your adulthood. This state of preconditioned dating is not often realized until later in life. But it can still be useful to you as you look back and tie together the past with the route to romance you took to get to where you are today. If your mother and father always yelled at home, this would become a norm and could possibly resurface in your relationships. These are learned behaviors that can be altered if you recognize them for what they are. Know yourself.

Your first experience of love typically comes from your

parents. People who come from loving homes are statistically better equipped to deal with relationships. They are well rounded and have a balanced perception on love and dating. This isn't to say that people from loving homes won't mess up because they probably will. They will just have a foundational head start on the rest of us. Lessons others learn the hard way, come from their parents and can essentially replicate once engaged in a relationship with someone just by tapping into their memory banks...I was not so fortunate. I saw my parents fight. I saw my mother cry. I saw my dad move on. I never met my dad's father because like my dad, he did not remain with his wife my grandmother.

A perpetual cycle of missing dads and hurting women. I became numb to the tears of women at an early age. Not because I didn't care but because I had seen it enough for it to no longer phase me. One of the earliest things that I learned about love was that people will leave you. This is not the greatest lesson to learn at four-years old. This is a lesson that some people in their 30s and beyond still don't get. I will spell it out: NOT EVERYONE

WILL LOVE YOU AND SOME OF THOSE THAT DO WILL

STILL LEAVE. Love does not mean they will stay, (or stay

faithful). I accepted it, unknowingly making it an option for a lot

of my relationships down the road. My best-friend's parents have

been (and still are) together for over 30 years. My best-friend's

relationships also have that same staying power. Contrarily, my

relationships had to be shaped that way because my natural

inclination was to leave because that's what I had seen my father

do.

My father doesn't know this because I don't think I ever told

him. I remember watching him leave, carrying his army green

duffle bag walking away from us. My mother and I. I remember

my mom crying in the doorway. I just wanted to make her happy.

This was another defining moment in my stages of love

development. I established a desire to make women happy. I

hated seeing my mom upset and later on I hated seeing other

women upset. As I grew into a teenager who was beginning to

discover girls, I noticed that the ones I seemed to gravitate

towards were "damaged". Girls who had been cheated on,

abused, been done wrong, or had low self-esteem. Girls who wanted a hero.

At this point I wasn't preying on a weakness but attempting to be their knight in shining armor. I would often joke about the world needing more of me. In my mind I had the ability to satisfy any woman. I was the perfect guy. I wanted to save them all. Little did I know, the saving they would need was saving from me.

Ex factor- *She embodied all of the traits that I felt I wanted in a woman; intelligence, beauty, and strength. All qualities that I felt would satisfy my desire for love and to be loved. I'll call her "the Athlete", a beautiful mixture of strength wrapped in a voluptuous layer of cream. Like steel caressed in silk, she was a beautiful but hardened woman. She had a past. So did I. We had met briefly in college and kept in touch years later after my departure. At this point in my life, I had begun to re-evaluate my stance on relationships. Bedding a different woman every night was starting to get old and I could sense my desire for the chase was beginning to wane. I was still discovering the traits* *that I felt would constitute an ideal lover for me to settle with. This is where "The Athlete" came in. I made plans to spend a weekend romancing her. I intended to wine and dine her, take her back home and reel her in with a night of intimacy. The plan went off without a hitch. The night was full of stimulating conversation, reminiscing about college shenanigans, future plans and more. We were close, we connected on multiple levels. It was all… perfect. At least it appeared that way.*

During the weekend of us getting to know each other, she had let me know that she had grown up as the oldest of six sisters raised by a tough father. Emotions were for sissies. Her dad had not raised any of those, so all of her qualities were right for me. But for her, being emotional, being vulnerable, opening up to someone else and letting them in was not something she had become comfortable with. Lesson learned. Needless to say history did not repeat itself with myself and "The Athlete".

Fools repeat history-Edmund Burke once said, that " those who don't know history are destined to repeat it." ALL relationships are learning experiences. If nothing else, you will at least gain the benefit of knowledge.

Each experience adds knowledge, because no matter how similar people seem, we are all different. Our inability to observe these lessons sets us up for failure. An important question to ask in any new relationship is, *How did the "old one" end?* If your purpose of pursuit is something more casual, then asking about the scope of the last situation and how it ended should be your course. Meaning learning the terms of their last situation, and whose decision it was to end it.

You should also note trends between your past and your present. Red flags make themselves known and we have the responsibility to notice them and take action. It is irresponsible and selfish not to learn from your past. Do not be that person. You'll end up not only destroying your chance for happiness but potentially someone else's.

Every day is a lesson- One thing you need to know how to do in regards to history is to just be able to recognize truth and keep a detailed record. Some people live life,others let life just happen. If you are one of the latter then relationships will always be devastating. You won't hold any control, and will end up being a puppet to anyone who decides to pull your strings. You're no different than someone who keeps trying to fill a strainer up with water. No matter how much is poured into you, in the end you remain empty. Do not deny what you see. Learn how someone acts and their strengths and weaknesses. Learn how you feel about these person's actions, and learn about your OWN strengths and weaknesses. Learn the power they hold over you and vice versa. No matter what it is, commit it to memory. Learn. Grow. Evolve.

Who we were determines who we will be.- Our past. It is the footprint that lead to our present and guides our future. When we appreciate our love history we can grow from it. We can shape ourselves into something meaningful. The things we grow from ultimately start us off on our love journey. Every experience that we encounter shapes how we perceive love in the future, as long as we are willing to learn and grow from it. A man who has been cheated on in an earlier relationship may have an aversion to commitment. This is something he should factor in when he attempts to date. A woman who had a lover pass away may hold unresolved feelings for him. Love is not clear and does not touch everyone the same. Who we were determines who we will be. However, there is always an opportunity to be more. In regard to love and relationships, we create a future based on our own past. Our love is unique to us all. It originated from a specific point in our lives that no one else can say they came from, yet how we share it affects everyone whom we encounter. You have to love past your own past so that you can have a stronger love in the future.

2

<u>Does it add up?</u>

Love is sometimes a game of numbers. You have to play the odds and check the statistics to find the best situation for you. When I say numbers I mean the predictive dating factors. Factors such as repetitive patterns (the ones that both you and the person you're pursuing exhibit), financial figures (not just the amount of money made, but the amount that is spent and wasted as well), as well as the number of people who play a role in your relationship.

In reality, dating usually requires very little thought and actually relies more on habit (hence why they are called dating habits) . We are working towards becoming BETTER lovers, and in doing so we have to be more conscientious of the decisions we make in regards to Love. Let's plug in the numbers and see where it takes us.

Dating Patterns: The odds are…- Patterns say a lot about a person. Patterns are typically reflective of an individuals dating choices. Specifically bad choices. If you want more success in your relationships, take a good hard look at "*your type*" then date the opposite.

The reason I say this is because if you can date a specific demographic enough for it to be considered a type, it's obviously not working for you. If bad boys are your *type,* you must have dated more than one to arrive at the conclusion that they are your type. However, staying with any *type* of person will yield the same results you received the first couple of times. In order to break that cycle, try something new.

Ex Factor.- *Two years into college, I had already made dozens of romantic mistakes, more so than most people at that age. I loved women who didn't deserve it. I had sex with women I had no intention of loving. I gave myself to woman after woman,* *most of which offered me the exact same emptiness that I had become so familiar with momentary bliss validated through physical action.*

I had convinced myself I wanted more than that. However I took no action toward the contrary. I had gotten used to the routine of seduce-and-conquer that had become the story of my life. I was broken. I couldn't see it, but I was a storm; breaking hearts and leaving more broken people in my wake.

I will call her "Red". The first thing she did to set herself apart was to connect with me on an intellectual level. I wasn't used to that. Most women I had dealt with were easily swayed by whatever nonsense that came out of my mouth. Dumb women were easy to manipulate. I could say the sky was green and they'd probably believe it.

"Red" had her own mind and I admired that about her. She also had an immense amount of self-respect. This became obvious when I couldn't bed her right away. Not only did she expect more of herself, but she also expected more of me.

So why, with all of these qualities, did I not jump for the opportunity to be with someone like this? Because she wasn't my

type . I had not yet learned that types *should be avoided. I*

wanted the familiar. Someone I knew how to control. She was

unexpected. New territory that I wasn't brave enough to venture

into. We connected physically once, but it wasn't enough to keep

her around. I realized that she was at a level I wasn't ready to be

at. Unable to shake old habits, and scared to create new trends, I

continued my pattern of bad dating for years to come.

Dating patterns are sometimes hard to decipher. Why am I attracted to the women I am attracted to? Why do all of my relationships end the same way? These patterns are usually defined in your history or your partner's.

However, recognizing the pattern is the first step. The acceptable answer is NOT, "That's just who I've always dated." If that is your response then you will continue to pull in losers who waste your time or whose time you waste. Evolve your thinking.

Your focus for this chapter is to identify patterns. Every person who dates has a pattern. Even if you think you do not have a pattern, you do. Your pattern can, in itself, be random. If you intentionally date someone different every time without establishing grounds for what you like and don't like, then you can never determine what is actually best for you. Relationships that you can not learn and grow from are pointless. You've wasted weeks, months, or years of your life and someone else's if the end result is you're the same as when you went into the relationship.

To identify your pattern, go to your dating history and analyze who you have been with. Was every guy you dated a "bad boy"? Did every girl you were involved with want commitment too fast? Did everyone you slept with never call back? These are the questions you need to ask.

If your list is long (like mine) do not go through every person you have ever dated. Instead, find a period in time such as your college years and build from there. Remember, the point of studying the factors of dating is to find predictive methods that you can use to shape your dating future.

Now that you have identified the pattern, isolate the variable that has caused the relationship to fail. All relationships have a defining moment that send it into a downward spiral. That is the variable. Just like in middle school algebra, your job is to solve for the unknown. Three relationships all ended with the same result: heartbreak.

In solving for the unknown (because that is what you are trying to do), take away the known elements, and you-are left with is the variable that continues to vex you. The known elements are the things that the people in your pattern do NOT have in common with you. Let me give you an example:

Sally - blonde, good job, goes to the gym, smoker, emotionless

Denise - redhead, unemployed (student), artist, smoker, supportive

Veronica - brunette, unstable job history, homebody, smoker, boring

Although all of these women may have both positive and negatives traits. However, what you're solving for is your variable. The commonality between these women is that they are all smokers. If all of these relationships were to fail, then you would need to re-evaluate how you approach dating and consider eliminating smokers from your dating pool.

This is a very lax example that gives you the idea of what you need to look for. We are creatures of habit, so it should not be hard to locate and isolate the element that has been causing your relationships to end. Do your homework. You can also use this same formula to solve for problems that exist in your relationship currently. Find the common denominator and remove it.

Common Denominators- In relationships, there are reoccurring traits. They occur for one of two reasons: (1) because you are either habitually dating, or (2) you do not approach each relationship with a dynamically fluid frame of mind. If repetitive actions occur in dating, then one of the two parties is the common denominator. Figure out if it is you or them, and find it quick.

Repetitive negative behavior has a psychological effect on your overall perception of the relationship. The more relationships you have that exhibit a particular behavior will only amplify the aversion you have towards that behavior. Meaning, what only somewhat bothered you about Tyrone, may bother you twice as much with James, and will bother you even more with Michael. Find these problems and address them immediately.

If the common denominator resides in you, you need to assess the information using the previous method of solving for the unknown. Change the focus. Instead of keying in on dating behaviors exhibited by others, take a look at the behaviors and emotions felt by yourself. Once you notice your mannerisms, learn how to work against your own programming and consciously try to be different. Evolve your thinking.

Prime Number Dating- A prime number is any number that can only be divided by one and itself. Dating should have the exact same properties. Generally speaking, dating works best if there are only two people involved. Do not involve your mother, your sister, your brother, your best friend, your uncle twice removed or the family dog in every decision that is made in your relationship. The more moving parts any object has, the more complicated it is to maintain. It is a lot easier to fix a 10-speed bike than it is to fix a Toyota Camry. Simplicity is the key to keeping relationships less stressful, attracting higher quality individuals, and merging your life with someone else's. For example, if you have a room that is already full and you are trying to put your treadmill in there, it will only fit once you remove something else. In the case of relationships, the treadmill represents other people. So do yourself a favor and keep it simple.

Gotta pay to play- Finances play a major part in your relationship as a whole. Finances are one of the major causes of relationship failure. Lack of finance plus differences in opinions on spending create financial inequalities and imbalances.

Not having money is a problem. Without money you cannot do anything without some sort of sponsor. You can't pay your bills, you can't take care of yourself, you can't have fun. The lack of finance creates a situation where you are struggling to live and makes having a relationship almost impossible. You cannot date without receiving the generosity of someone else. Stabilize your finances before you attempt to date.

Differences in Opinion on Spending – He wants to buy a boat, you want to start a savings fund. She wants to go shopping, he wants to pay bills. These things are important to know if you plan to have a serious relationship (or anything beyond a one night stand). How your partner spends money can have a direct impact on *your* money. If your live-in girlfriend blows $1,000 at the mall and has no money to help with the bills, guess who has to pick up the slack? If you have any intentions of continuing to date someone, make sure you have an idea of their spending habits.

Financial Inequalities and Imbalances-Some of these factors can be controlled and some cannot. It may not be your fault that your wife makes $80,000 a year and you make $40,000. But that inequality has an effect on the way the two view money. I know a lot of men who, even though their woman has a considerable income, will not allow her to assist them financially and would rather struggle to work two jobs to take care of the home. It's not the 1950's. I'm not saying she should be paying the bulk, but she can pay a phone bill or something. Financial imbalances come when one person contributes more financially than the other. Therefore, if a couple both brings home the same $50,000 a year, but one person applies the majority of their income to bills; while the other spends it frivolously, then there is destined to be a problem. Understand the possible differences in finances between you and your lover and come up with a plan that works for you both.

THE DATING ALGORITHM

1. Assess yourself.

2. Assess the person you are dating (or trying to date).

3. Create a formula that works for both of you.

4. Keep your formula.(Repeat)

3

<u>Sticks and Stones...</u>

Communication is probably the biggest roadblocks to any relationship's success. Not being able to put into words how you feel and expecting your lover to "just know" is common. As sweet as the idea of your lover being able to complete your sentences and sense every issue without it being said, truthfully if you don't speak on it, you will probably be overlooked. The failure to do this does not mean your partner does not care. Not everyone gets the same cues, so it is our responsibility to make sure the message is delivered.

Words are powerful. We never know how the words we choose will affect someone. Whoever said, "Sticks and stones will break my bones, but words will never hurt me," never experienced any real human interaction. Words can pierce you like nothing else and can stay with you much longer. Even the things we DON'T say but communicate nonverbally have an impact. Control what you communicate to have a better handle on your relationships. All interaction has an effect. It's up to you to determine what kind of effect it has.

Ex Factor - *I had always heard communication is important. Beyond just talking, there had to be a level of understanding, a meeting of the minds. At least to some degree people have to see eye-to-eye. You may not agree, but you should at least understand the other person's point of view.*

I struggled with this concept because most of the time I had dealt with women who were emotionally motivated and lacked the logic necessary to understand where I was coming from. Half of the time they didn't understand their own feelings. I didn't have too many women who I could speak to for long lengths of time about any subject. Until I met "The Muse".

I was around 24 years old. She was a good decade my senior. This was not my first encounter with an older woman. I had become accustomed to the company of older women because they had a higher level of maturity than women my age . To meet someone who possessed an inkling of maturity as well as intelligence was a treat.

We had connected online and made plans to engage in a night of enjoying the arts. We went to a little spot I knew that did poetry and got lost in thoughts of free expression. Engaged in thoughtful conversation, I felt like I could speak freely with her because she expected nothing from me. She was well aware of our differences in age and the different places we were in our lives. There was no judgement between us. She heard me. And the fact that she was listening to me caused me to actively listen to her. This was the first time that I felt like someone could have been a friend first before a lover.

The physical and emotional aspects of our developing relationship were also noteworthy. The sophisticated communication and our ability to connect on a parallel level was a game changer for me. That experience stayed with me long after we stopped seeing each other. It became a new criteria for what I would expect from "The One".

Love Language Barriers - If you were dropped off in Vietnam and wanted to ask a woman on a date who didn't speak English, how would you accomplish this? Although not so extreme many people engage others with the same set up.

When determining if someone is a match for you, you need to assess their compatibility. A huge part of compatibility is how you perceive and receive Love. The way you Love is not necessarily the same as the next person, so when you feel you are not being heard, it may not be an issue of biological hearing, but one of comprehension.

We have all witnessed the struggle when an American worker approaches a foreign customer, and instead of trying to clarify what they mean to say, they just yell what they said the first time. "Can I take your order?" becomes "CAN I TAKE YOUR ORDER!?" and the same confusion remains. When you feel like someone is not following you, saying or doing the same thing does not increase understanding. Instead, try to rework your message into one they will understand. Patience is the key to communicating effectively. Not everyone perceives or receives Love the same. Find the barriers that block effective communication and tear them down.

<u>Two Ears and One Mouth</u> – Listen. Listen often. Listen more than you talk, and be observant, even when things seem normal. Pay attention to yourself and your Lover. Don't overlook messages you are given, no matter how subtle. This lesson is the follow-up to breaking you're your barriers. Once you realize people communicate their feelings differently, you need to readjust your antennae so you can pick up on the things you would have missed before.

Listening and observing serve two purposes: inform and confirm. All relationships, whether serious or casual, have truths, facts, and knowledge that are passed between the two parties. We create messages both verbal and nonverbal which convey these messages to our Lover. When listening or observing, determine whether you are seeking to inform or confirm.

By *inform, I mean* in the sense of gaining or seeking new knowledge. To confirm I mean to satisfy a known suspicion or a preconceived belief. "How was your day?" is a simple question that should always be taken as an opportunity to absorb information. What your partner does or does not say speaks volumes. Try not to respond until after all of the information has been received. First, because speaking or acting prior to the conclusion of their disclosure shows a lack of respect and will most likely incite an unfavorable response ; secondly, you may prevent yourself from hearing something important.

Nonverbal Communication - What is not said is sometimes more important than what is. This is when observation is important. Couples usually falter in this area of communication. Women tend to see men's actions (nonverbal) as a form of communication, even if no message is being relayed. Men, on-the-other-hand, tend not to capture nonverbal elements. Interpretation is not usually the primary mode of communication for men, therefore, messages that are being given are overlooked. Women usually are not satiated by simple answers offered by their male counterparts and men tend to be less perceptive to things that are not clearly stated. How do you make the most out of nonverbal communication? Learning how people communicate comes with observing them and committing their behaviors to memory. Controlling and being aware of your body language and nonverbal communication will also help set the tone for acceptable behaviors. Pay attention.

Say it Like You Mean it - All too often, messages are distorted because we speak and communicate with the consideration of others. However with no consideration at all, we stand the chance of sending a message that falls on deaf ears. Tact is definitely important anytime you convey a message. However, when you soften your words it can also soften the meaning. The goal should be to deliver a message that is clear and concise, without raising barriers.

Ask yourself the following questions before delivering any message:

1) **Am I being clear about what my wants, needs and desires?**
Making sure our message is easily comprehended is important. Saying, "I need some space," can have multiple meanings. Do you want a few hours out at a bar? Or do you need a longer period

of separation?

2) **How will the receiving party likely react to what I'm about to say?** Anticipating a reaction is good preparation for any message whether good news or bad. Even if you don't EXPECT IT, be prepared for fallout if it's bad news.

3) **Does my method of transmission show consideration for the receiving party?** How you deliver a message is important. Texting someone versus a face-to-face discussion can have two completely different responses to the same message.

4) **Am I picking the right time to deliver this message?** Timing is everything. A huge part of tact is not just knowing what to say, but when to say it. Telling your girlfriend you want to see other people right after her mom gets diagnosed with cancer is never good.

Message You Want to Relay: "Your weight gain is concerning me."

Wrong Way: "You're fat."

Better Way: "I've noticed you've put on a few pounds. Would you like to join me at the gym?"

Remember, compatibility and the continuity of a relationship are both heavily fortified by the ability of both parties to communicate. Eliminate language barriers, listen more than you speak, be aware of nonverbal communication; and always deliver effective and honest messages. Communication is the nervous system of any relationship. Without it, your relationship cannot function properly.

4

The Lover's Law of

Attraction

What drives us to chase the people we desire? What makes us appealing to another person? The laws of attraction that govern our actions are not much different than nature's laws of attraction. We are the products of a natural environment after all, and therefore, we should exhibit the same characteristics others within that environment do. A lot of things I'm going to describe that define our level of attraction are not new concepts in life, only in Love. We know the cliché sayings like "opposites attract" and "birds of a feather flock together," but this all just scratches the surface. The science of relationships, which for most people require a lot of experimentation, can be simplified into a tried and true method for natural selection for Love and relationships.

For something to be a law it must be unable to be disproven. No matter what factors and variables are used, it must always garner the same result. The first law of attraction you need to establish for yourself is actually the one that negates attraction. These are easy to describe since most people can easily state what components they don't want in a relationship. Going back through your Love history lesson you can find the things you have determined won't work for you. Although you hate to admit it, these "won't work for you" people are usually your "type".

When dating, most of you tell yourselves that you have a type. However if you have dated a certain demographic enough for it to be considered a type, it obviously can't be working for you. Otherwise, you would have only dated one or two, which would not characterize a dating trend. We often overlook actual signs of attraction when it doesn't fit the trend and miss out on the thing that compliments us romantically.

Define the elements that are detrimental to your relationship . Keep in mind, these elements need to be definite and not things that you prefer not to have. For example, dating someone with kids may not be ideal, but if you are open to it under certain circumstances, it will not qualify for an item of repulsion. But if smoking is a definite no, in any circumstance that would be an item of repulsion. As you gather this list of things that would definitely be a deal breaker for a relationship, you begin to focus your search in the Land of Love. Before your time is wasted, assess and progress effectively and keep your romantic timeline clean, free of any unnecessary Lovers.

Ex Factor - *It was my second year in college and my reputation had grown. Men envied and respected me for the number of women I had been with. Women desired me and were curious to see if there was any truth to the hype. I had become the campus Casanova. It was my reputation that sent women running to my bed room , just not ones I could grow with. Regardless of what people believed about me, I was not this amazing ladies'* man. I simply found a way to make my search for Love look planned out. But I was failing miserably.

I told myself that if I was going to find Love I would have to approach things differently. I would have to find someone who was different from my norm, because opposites attract, (as the saying goes). That year I ran into "The Pretender" and thought she was the one who could bring change into my life. That was a huge mistake on my part.

We dated and I discovered that she was my polar opposite in almost every way. We clashed a lot, and really, the only thing keeping us together was her craving for physical intimacy, which I gave to her.

WHAT YOU HAVE

WHAT YOU NEED   WHAT YOU WANT

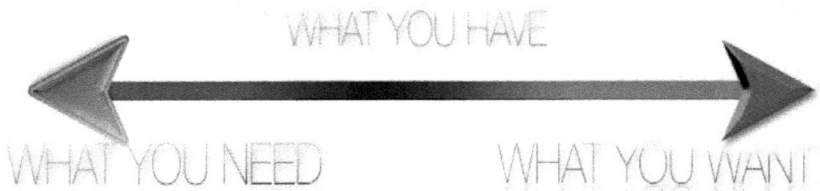

To the core of my being I wanted to make things work with her. Not because of who she was, but because I was at a point in my life where I felt like if I can't make this relationship work I would never find anyone. I held on, until the point of insanity. We were nothing alike. We weren't just opposites, we were opposing forces, and as our relationship went down in flames I felt like I had tried to trick myself into believing I could be happy. Soon after, I reverted to my previous ways. Love them and leave them. It was easier that way.

<u>Affinity</u>- Occasionally, you come across an individual we are undoubtedly drawn to. It's a spontaneous or natural attraction or sympathy for someone or something. -Like the sun's gravitational pull, the attraction is greater than your ability to resist. They pull you in and set you ablaze. It happens on a biological level, one you cannot understand, nor do you try to. There is just....*something* about this object of your desire that you find appealing. Being attracted to women with long hair, or men with muscles, or someone who is at least six feet tall, or who speaks another language, or who is intelligent, or drives a certain type of car. These things all seem necessary because we give them priority but in reality they are not. These attractions fall on the *want* end of the spectrum.

Liken it to good food. We feel it is necessary for food to taste good, and have come to expect it, but satisfying flavors are just a benefit. Truth is, succulence is an enhancer. The purpose of food is to provide fuel for the body. In the same way, these aspects of desirability that draw us in are not necessary components, but are the spices that gives the basis of what we really need. These superficial factors are the flavor to our relationship's necessities. In essence, a relationship broken down to bare bones would have mental, physical, emotional, financial, and spiritual stability. Anything provided beyond that is a bonus. So don't get hung up on her long flowing hair that she had when you two first met. It has been my experience that a lot of women will cut their hair to give themselves a different aura. Or, that six pack that he had when he was 21; 10 years and two kids later it may not be as tight. However, if these things do provide significance, prioritize them as "important wants" and do not give them the same attention as a need.

Magnetism and Polar aAttraction- A negative pole will pull toward a positive one and will push away from one that is alike. People can operate in much the same way. This works when you have couple that complement each other.

NOT ALL OPPOSITES ATTRACT. Remember it like this: complimentary aspects that are opposite tend to attract. Opposites attract when they are capable of enhancing each other. But even in doing so they must adjust to fit one another in order to bring out the best in each other. This means that the two individuals must take on characteristics of the other and vice versa. In chemistry when two elements combine they must share certain components of the same molecules. The strength of that bond is reflected by how many electrons they share. The sharing of electrons is the molding of the element to fit another. Being malleable in relationships increases your chances of finding a **LOVE THAT WORKS.**

Homogamy- Homogamy is a term that means people tend to marry those who are like themselves: socioeconomic status, religious identity, and cultural identity. These factors are determinants for compatibility and lean more toward the *need* end of the spectrum. This is an example of the "birds of a feather" sentiment, and in a lot of regards this remains true. The two main reasons why this is true is because of the specific lifestyle needs of each individual and how people of the same type usually occupy the same circles. You can choose anyone in the world you want, but not just anyone will fit into your world. This counters the belief that opposites attract and usually is found in people looking for mature lasting relationships.

Lifestyle Love Needs -Lifestyle Love needs are

conditions that we have in place, specific to the way we live, and would be required in a romantic relationship. A woman with two kids will need certain things from a man in order to consider him ideal. A man who has a thriving but demanding career may need a woman who is flexible and goal oriented. We determine the wants, and life determines the needs. Thus, resolving a need from a want helps to clear out the clutter of your Love life. Our overall attraction level is a combination of our wants and needs but for the similarity cause, our wants are usually eclipsed by our needs.

P.O.A: Point of Attraction- We all possess Point of Attraction (P.O.A.) and it is a weakness of sorts. The P.O.A. is one thing that pulls us in more than anything. It creates a reaction on every level we can think of. It is quantifiable, and can be measured out by the actions with which we use in its pursuit.

Although there are many factors that dictate why we date, chase, and get involved with who we do, the P.O.A. is a key factor that can have a major impact on your Love life. It is the hole in our heart's defenses, allowing people to slip past what would usually be guarded. A person's P.O.A. can be simple, (e.g. a guy with dimples; or a woman with long hair). Or it can be complex, (e.g. a guy with a defined set of goals; or a woman with an established career). Now, do not simply see a P.O.A. as something you find attractive about someone. Think of it more as a dart board; with your point of attraction being your Bull's eye.

P.O.A. varies from person to person, but we all have them. You can usually tell if it is your P.O.A. if you can overlook other negative traits because of the presence of one particular appealing trait. Whether in a relationship or casually dating this characteristic, if held by the one we are involved with, becomes an Achilles heel in our love life. This   kind of attraction is dangerous because it is reactionary. It can also be used as a tool for those who wish to seduce someone. Understanding someone's P.O.A. can give you the upper hand when trying to engage them. For example: you know that a woman's P.O.A. is a man who is good with kids. In order to appeal to her, you would place yourself in situations where you can exhibit that trait, (even if only falsified for the sake of getting what you want).

It is always ideal to guard your P.O.A. If people know

how to tug at your desires they can manipulate you. For example, if a man is a sucker for a woman who is a good kisser, than that woman needs only the power of lips to get her way. There is an offensive and defensive side to dating. But before you can start establishing game plans, you must first know what is attractive to you.

We often say we can't help who we are attracted to. Superficially, this is true. We are products of our surroundings and at times fighting what seems natural is impossible. However, being attracted and succumbing to attraction are two different things. Having a keen understanding of who you are attracted to and why will give you a deeper understanding as to why your relationships operate the way they do. There is a science to it… but it is not rocket science.

5

Can't fight Nature

Love is a funny thing sometimes. Relationships today are a mixture of fairytales, technology, rumors and half-truths where everyone is loving nobody and somebody's loving everybody. Love is both living and manmade . It is stationary and evolving. Because there are so many cogs that make it go, we have to accept both the natural and unnatural elements and understand how each affect us.

We are natural beings in an unnatural world. There are so many outside factors that play a part in our relationships. Human beings, like any other animal (and yes, we are animals) have to survive in any environment and must be able to adapt and evolve.

The strong will survive and the weak will be weeded out. Natural selection in relationships will always favor the traits deemed most favorable for the conditions they are under. However, nothing is set in stone. It is never too late to grow into something more beautiful (or more dangerous if thats is what your desire) in the field of Love. It is time to tame the animal of Love.

At all times there are forces at work in a relationship: natural, manmade, internal and external. How we react to these forces determine the quality of our current and future relationships .

Internal- Internal elements, or factors, occur actively between two people in a relationship and are acted upon . These elements usually present themselves in the form of character traits or behaviors and actions exhibited by one individual or the other. Earlier in The Lover's Man-ual, I spoke on the presence of conflicting forces in relationships. This happens whenever two people come together as the differences between them sort themselves out. If they cannot sort themselves out then they will ultimately fall apart. For example; when a newly married couple discovers one member is bad with money. Although the one may be bad with money, this is an internal force that affects the relationship as a whole. . Internal forces are the easiest to control because they happen between the members of the relationship.

External- External forces that act independently of the relationship but still affect the overall outcome. External factors are constantly present and constantly playing a role in your love life. These are things as small as someone cutting your boyfriend off in traffic, which causes him to be short with you when he gets home. Or they can be as serious as a death in the family that has a lasting effect on one or both members of the relationship. External forces are not at all able to be controlled by you or your lover. Understanding this fact is important in how you handle your relationship. The following are two examples of external factors playing a role in a relationship:

Scenario 1: Girlfriend, while borrowing the brand new car of her Lover, is rear ended in a parking lot. Upon hearing the news, Boyfriend is furious and begins yelling. Arguments ensue and the relationship now has to manage both internal and external factors that are acting upon it.

Scenario 2: Girlfriend, while borrowing the brand new car of her Lover is rear ended in the parking lot. Upon hearing the news, boyfriend realizes external factors (such as someone else hitting the car) are unavoidable and outside of his control. He tells his girlfriend not to worry and he is glad she is okay. They have sex.

Natural- Natural factors are things that occur without provocation as a result of biological, psychological or some other somatic process. People, being that they are animals, must succumb to what happens naturally within the body: sleep, food, touch and the release of endorphins in response to it. Height, weight, and aging are all things that are naturally occurring and typically, from our perspective, have a minimal effect on our relationships. However, this is a very foundational aspect because naturally occurring forces make us who we are. How your wife acts throughout the day can be shifted by the chemical imbalances that are created from depriving the body of certain bodily needs. How your significant other deals with you as they age could change based upon the body and how it handles the aging process. The male physiology and the female physiology both create scenarios in which there may be opposing forces that must be dealt with. Like the age old question of who gets to determine what the thermostat setting will stay on. These forces are somewhat within our control but the effects of which are not as easily noticed . Therefore discussing things like family health history, eating habits, sleeping patterns and more can give you insight into the forces that act upon your †Lover as well as yourself.

Manmade - Manmade forces act upon relationships in the form of technology and devices that do not have a part in the natural environment. According to an article posted by ABC news, Divorce Online found that Facebook appeared in over 75% of all divorce filings in the United States in 2011 and is listed as the cause in almost a third of them. That may seem shocking but it goes to show the importance people place on "things". [1]

Now, that was a negative statistic but that does not mean that all manmade forces are negative. For a soldier deployed overseas, he may be able to keep his relationship intact due to his ability to Skype with his girlfriend every day. Manmade forces and their effects are determined by a couple's aversion to using them. When you have one person in love with social media and another who hates it, the presence of social media will drive a wedge between the two. It is great to discuss with your Lover (if it is serious enough to do) how they feel about cell phones, social media, and other media outlets that are on the rise in our society and can play a part in how your relationship continues.

Just as with Newton's Laws of Motion, whether your relationship goes forward, backward or stops is dependent on the forces that act upon it. However, in your relationship, you have the ability to minimize the effect that these forces have by identifying them as they are and adapting. Do not allow forces to move your relationship without understanding why.

All living creatures naturally adapt. That is to say, when a creature is put in a certain situation, given circumstances, they create outcomes that are more favorable for survival. So why do we not do the same in relationship? The creatures that do not evolve die off. And the same can be said of relationships that do not adapt to the ever changing environment. Whether the scenario is good or bad you must be willing to accept, interpret, and adapt to the forces that are thrust upon your relationship. Make Love work for you. Evolve your relationship.

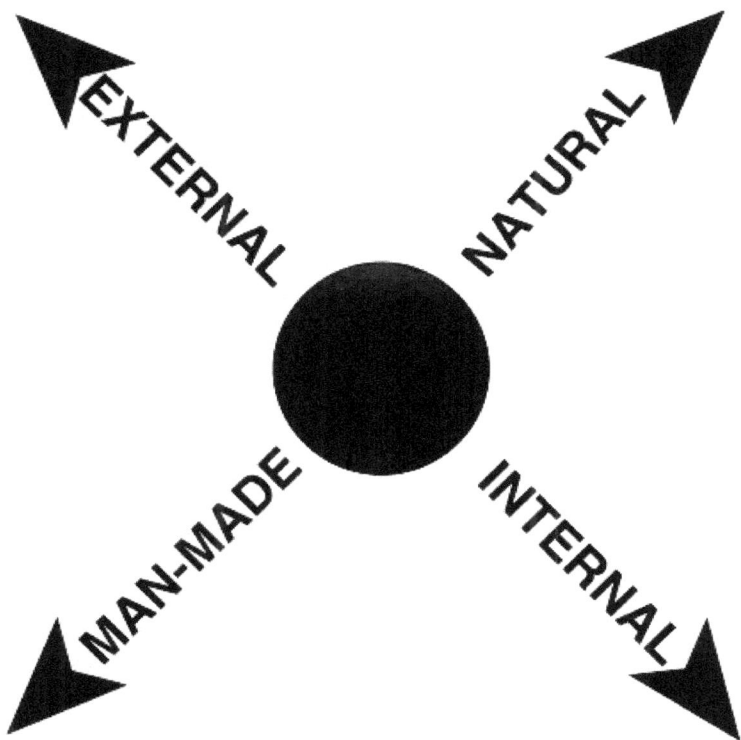

EXTERNAL NATURAL MAN-MADE INTERNAL

6

The Circle of Love

Everyone has wants, needs, and desires. We cannot fight it; it is in our nature. Attraction is powerful. No matter how much we try to pretend we don't "need" anyone, our hearts and bodies yearn to make connections. I'm not sure if you can isolate love on a subatomic level but it appears to be built into our DNA...to Love and be Loved.

But often we succumb to the power of love instead of harnessing it to suit our needs. Love is powerful. The emotional, mental, physical, and spiritual aspects of it are what shape everyday actions. Just the idea of knowing that one person can make the world fade away in a moment of bliss with just a touch or a kiss; it is enough to satiate the average Lover. When Love happens, you are actually fading into your lover. You get sucked into the vacuum that is their Love void. You fight to fill that empty space and try to be everything they need. In turn you lose the concept of your needs. You become a victim instead of a victor. Essentially, you have become Love's whipping boy, and although it makes for a great R&B song, being someone's Love slave is an awful situation. No more! It's time to become an evolved Lover.

Becoming the best Lover you can be requires discipline, patience, and knowledge. It is not about sexual ability, being a great lover is an art. It is tactical, it is strategic and it is purposeful. Being a great lover is not a matter of chance occurrences. You make the bed with which your suitors will want to lay.

When people speak of Love and war as separate entities, they really mean to compare the similarities. In finding companionship there will be conflict. The goal is to make this conflict one that is manipulated or predictable by you and an outcome that favors your desires. Taking care of yourself first is smart, not selfish. If you neglect to make yourself happy, how can you make someone else happy? Being a better lover will in turn create a situation in which you start to come out on top when managing all of your relationships. Your love will conquer all.

We have already established that you must have an understanding of who you are. The next step is taking that information and determining how you love. Not everyone loves the same or process love the same way. You need to be able to recognize how people express their Love and how you express yours. You will have certain expectations and will hold people to them whether they know it or not. The way you Love is generally based off how you were shown Love and your personality qualities.

My experiences have taught me that there are a variety of different lovers that exist in the world. At any given time a person can exhibit traits from multiple types, however, there are essentially three categories of Lovers . (1) There are the *physical Lovers* who express desire through physical intimacy. They appeal to and attract others by action and are motivated by the idea of receiving the same. (2) There are the *intellectual Lovers*. They see love as a calculated set of events that are triggered by cause-and-effect. They are stimulated by understanding others and use conversation as their tool of seduction. Lastly, (3) there are *emotional Lovers*. Those who act based on their feelings, no matter how fleeting. Emotional Lovers are spontaneous and can seem erratic at times, but that is all a part of their appeal. Like a checks and balances system, each form of Love is succumbed to another. Physical action cannot sway a Lover who has a logical understanding of how and why they do what they do. On-the-other-hand, the intellectual Lover is left clueless as to the reasoning and logic behind a Lover driven purely on emotion. And the emotional Lover is constantly placed under the power of the physical Lover, whose physical acts, whether good or bad, always cause an emotional reaction. No form of Love is better than another and no one is subject to one form. Evolving as a person and switching your style to fit the situation will help you be able to maneuver and manipulate yourself and others into the optimal place for your heart, mind and body to get what it wants and needs. You are in control. You may hear me mention the types again later. Different lessons may need to be approached from all three perspectives. From my own personal accounts of lust and Love, I will convey the knowledge I have acquired that made me the Lover I am today. Perfection comes not from solidarity, but from confidence . Being a well rounded Lover is an essential part to being the best Lover you can be.

P-Lovers - Physical Lovers, or P-Lovers, are those who associate love with physical action or touch. They are doers. For them, image is usually everything: a man who spends a lot of time in the gym and loves showing off the fruits of his labor or a woman with natural "gifts" who chooses to wear revealing clothes to put herself on display. P-Lovers enjoy being viewed by their partner and seen with their partner. Compliments are always welcome. Actually it is almost a requirement. They tend to focus more so on themselves, not in a self-centered way, but in a display of confidence . For example, if they are hungry they may say, "I want pizza," and invite you to their favorite pizza place. P-

Lovers are assertive and may sometimes overlook minuscule details of the relationship.

They can also be the ones to fall into routines. As long as there is the perception of love, change is not necessary. They try and buy your affection. Most people see this as a negative, but understand, they have a different understanding of affection. Do not cast them away for this reason alone. P-Lovers are the ones who "move fast" . To them, in order for it to be real it must be tangible. Physical intimacy is a necessity and removing this aspect can result in them ultimately walking away. You must have the right "touch" when you are with a P-Lover. Good sex and constant affection will satisfy any P-Lover.

E-Lovers - E-Lovers, or emotional Lovers are the romantics. Love is not an extension for them as it is for the other types of Lovers. Rather, an E-Lover exists for their love. E-Lovers seem to never be alone. In fact, you would probably recognize them as the kind of Lover who jump from one relationship to the next. Being alone is not an option. They are malleable, transforming constantly and evolving to fit into the life of the one they desire. They are the artists, the creative ones, who are in touch with their emotions and have a uniquely romantic perception of life and Love. They value love and see it as a precious gem to be treasured. They suffer from emotional overload, often causing them to appear erratic and unstable. They require stability, which is usually only given by their lover. They show their Love through big sweeping gestures and are the ones to fight hardest for Love. They are supportive but tend to need the their partner to achieve a higher level of personal satisfaction.

I-Lovers - I-Lover, or intellectual Lovers, are the students of Love. They are the thinkers. Love is broken down into cause and effect. For them, two things are important: knowing and having control. Having an understanding of what is happening creates a sense of comfort for the I-Lover. For example, while an E-Lover may accept someone's words when they say, "I love you," an I-Lover would equate an imbalance of words and actions that do not match.

I-Lovers are content with being single and actually take a long time to develop a relationship. This is because relationships must be rationalized. They are the "controllers" of the relationship, but not in a manipulative way. In order to maintain the upper hand and not being taken advantage of. They are usually the final word. They break up, make up and more…when they say so.

I-Lovers tend to have trust issues as they tend to overanalyze the details of their relationship focusing on and isolating any inconsistencies. They express love eloquently through words. They are the conversationalist; the type to have long meaningful talks with. They portray the image of someone who has got it together and usually work to keep it that way. They see love as a formula and if the equation is not balanced, they will quickly remove the uncommon denominator. Capturing their interest is essential. Stimulate the mind in order to gain entry into the heart. If you explore the world and expand their minds, an I-Lover will love you forever

Your love style will determine the *way* you love and the type of people you are drawn to. In this Cycle of love, people will either look for types that are like theirs or that succumb to their styles.

When you first meet someone you are interested in you...?

A. assess the situation carefully before making a move= Intellectual Lover

B. flirt shamelessly until they show interest back=Emotional Lover

C. place yourself within their view so that they notice you and hope they approach.= Physical Lover

When confronted with a problem in your relationship, your way of approaching it is...?

A. weighing the options and discussing solutions.= Intellectual Lover

B. dropping it because you don't want to be mad anymore.= Emotional Lover

C. make up sex= Physical Lover

Your idea of the perfect date is...?

A. long talks and stimulating conversation.= Intellectual Lover

B. something that doesn't really matter as long as you have your Lover.= Emotional Lover

C. one that ends up with the two of you sweating under the bed sheets.= Physical Lover

Ex Factor- *I will call her "The Void". It was 2007 and I was a 27-year-old home from college and working two jobs during the day while continuing my exploits with women at night. I had become a ghetto Casanova of sorts, thriving from my encounters with multiple women but I was still searching for "The One". It could be compared to car shopping. You test drive a few of them until you find the one you like. You may walk on a lot and see a car you know you are not going to buy. But the car gets up to 200 mph on the dash and you don't want to pass up the opportunity to get behind the wheel and give it a spin. Life was intimately interesting at this point in my life. I had no regrets.*

As time went and the summer closed I had connected with this oddity of a woman. What made her odd was her perception on love and relationships. She was someone who lacked the substance necessary to keep a guy interested. She was constantly

complaining of men leaving her and how they only wanted her for

sex. Unfortunately, sex was all she really had to offer, and not

even great sex at that. She was physically appealing but lacked in

everything else. She was a human doll with no concept of what it

meant to be someone's lover.

She always made sure her hair, nails and make-up were on point.

She had a seductive exterior with nothing on the inside,

especially in her head. She would often try to class-up sex by

using candles and music and incense to make herself feel like it

mattered more, knowing all too well that I would leave before the

sun came up. I humored her, slowing down my movements to give

a false sense of lovemaking. Lovemaking is not something that is

created by atmosphere, but as a more seasoned lover, I had

learned these things were necessary at times. Like a softer touch

to receive the pleasure I desired She was a place holder, a body

to kill time with. Just someone to see when I had the urge to fulfill

some basic desire.

At this point in my life I was colder and more emotionally

distant. I distrusted women as I had been cheated on, seemingly

without reason multiple times. Therefore, each encounter with
"The Void" was very deficient in conversation and foreplay. I
vaguely remember her getting upset with me one time because I
walked in her apartment and went straight to the bedroom.
Feeling hurt she asked me what it was she could do to take this
relationship to a more serious level. I looked her in the eyes and
told her flatly, "You aren't my type."

Now many people wonder how you can be sexually involved with someone who isn't your type. First, understand that sex is not indicative of how someone feels about you. A lot of women and some men mistake physical intimacy as proof that their Lover's care. Sex is a physical act. A guy can have sex with someone he has been friends with for years because he needs to get his rocks off, and a woman can have sex with a man they cannot stand FOR YEARS. Sex is sex. It can be more it can be less but assuming that it is something more simply because it happened will result with you getting played.

My agenda at the time was avoid having a serious relationship. I recognized "The Void's" method of love to be a physical one. Although she verbally would say she wanted emotional love, she expressed her love through physical action. Do not go solely by what people say. Go by their actions and how they react to you. Having a kitchen doesn't mean you can cook. Pay attention to their actions. Your love style dictates how you display your love. Words are just just words, but *how* you love is directly correlated to your love style.

"The Void" was no different. She would do her make-up and wear sexy lingerie and do whatever else she had to do to be visually appealing in order to stimulate a physical response from me. At the time I was an I-Lover, so no matter what she would do physically, I had already found the logic in what she was trying to do. She could have given me the best sex I ever had but it would not have mattered because my love style was going to trump hers.

In assessing your own love style, it is actually better to ask the opinions of others. Most people want to put themselves in certain categories. Being an intelligent person doesn't make you an intellectual lover. Love has its own rules which you will learn through this book. If you cannot be honest with yourself make a list of three people you dated in the past, not a current

relationship. Determine who had the power in the relationship

and understand why. If your ex was constantly getting into

trouble and knew they could get out of it by kissing you and

turning you on, they were a physical lover. If every time you and

your ex argued you always felt dumb or confused, it was probably

because they were an intellectual Lover. If you constantly felt

frustrated because everything was about how your ex felt and you

could not understand those feelings,you had yourself an

emotional Lover.

Everyone has a Love style. Knowing this should be one of

your first priorities when you establish a relationship . This also

works when evaluating friendships. Does this person operate with

physical intimacy, or is "knowing" what matters to them? Or

maybe they have an overly strong need to feel something?

Whatever the case, it is important to know what style they have

and know what style would be most compatible for you. Some

people can transition between styles with ease. For example, I

can go between physical and intellectual but struggle with being emotional. Before trying to control your Love style you must first understand all of the styles.

I-Lovers should avoid anyone who causes you to act without thinking. Your intellectual nature causes you to act based on what you know. Because physical Lovers move so fast they often don't give you time to think. Also, because emotional Lovers demand a certain level of Love and attention, they may be impatient with the thought processes of an I-Lover. However, this is your sanctuary, think things through. You are safe in relationships as long as you take the time to think and process whats is going on.

P-Lovers should avoid people who try to contain them. Emotional Lovers try to contain their Lovers with things like jealousy or anger. In order to keep their partners in place, emotional Lovers will express outbursts that physical Lovers want to avoid. Emotional Lovers will yell and scream and make you regret going out wearing an outfit that was too sexy,or having lunch with a coworker who is too attractive. Intellectual Lovers will make your advances seem meaningless. The sexual antics that had others begging for more does nothing to stir them up. Intellectual Lovers realize how important physical action is for P-Lovers and will try to diminish that by brushing you off. P-Lovers can only be themselves when they feel free to act on their urges, physical and otherwise. Continue to be assertive, state your desires to the one you are with and if they are against it, keep it moving.

E-Lovers need to avoid people who seem to always get you riled up. An intellectual Lover who has wised up to an emotional Lover may try to trigger an emotional response out of them to confuse them. If you are an E-Lover, a physical Lover will push your buttons through touch. Physical Lovers can have you eating out the palm of their hand if you are not careful. Instead, work to understand your own emotional triggers. Grow comfortable with situations in which you "allow" people to cause a response. Wear your emotions like a badge of honor, not of shame.

Understand that some people will try and dictate how you love. Don't let them get you out of your element. If you allow them to do this, it won't work. Your Love style is what comes natural to you, based on the point you are at in your life. You can change when you want to, but it is usually not successfully when someone else is the reason behind the change. Your lover may try to belittle you for not loving them the way they want you to, but don't let it sway you.. They may make statements like, "You don't understand me," or "I just want to show you the way I want to be loved." Everyone has a way they want to be loved, but it must coincide with the Love style that you exhibit. A fish is not dumb because it does not know how to walk on land, that is not what a fish was designed for. How we express our Love is no different. Not everyone's method is the same, but different doesn't mean wrong.

E-Lover P-Lover I-Lover L-Lover

7

<u>Cages</u>

Have you ever been with someone that seems to always bring the relationship down. Who was never satisfied with anything you did, and always criticized your every move? Or maybe you have been involved with someone who is so one sided with their viewpoints that they can't see the potential light at the end of the tunnel and their focus is always on the negative aspects of something? Most of us have, and a lot of the time it causes us to feel like we are the problem. Well I'm here to tell you that there are people who sabotage relationships and claim the victim role. Some of you may have experienced this and some of you may not understand what I mean. Just know that there are people who, when relationships seem too good to be true, will try to ruin it to gain some sense of reality. Because to them, the "fantasy" is unreal.

We Create Our Own Cages - Do not misunderstand, these people do not intend to be this way. Their perception of relationships has already been warped and they are in limbo between finding their identity and forgetting their past. These people have a hard time letting go and will tend to be the ones who date the same person on-and-off again or date a variety of different people in a short time period. Or if a new relationship fails, they will go back to a previous one because it is familiar. These relationships are poisonous for many reasons. These kind of Lovers realize they are damaged but do not want to appear that way. They put on the mask so that people don't recognize the potential headache that comes with dating them. The mask does more than hide who they are, it locks them in a world where their own happiness terrifies them. They have been hurt before, the cage they have built keeps the pain out but it ends up locking them in.

Ex Factor - *I was 22 and had just started a new career in healthcare. By this time I had established a name for myself as an amazing lover at my college, but this was a new environment, and a new opportunity. I didn't want my love affairs following me here. Not to mention, my reputation had grown to a point where setting up the perfect scenario for myself had become difficult. It was hard to build mystery and intrigue with women because they had already heard the legend of who I was and what I could do. So this time I tried something different. This is where my style switched from physical to intellectual.*

Finding women was never an issue for me. I worked in a female dominated workplace, a haven for any man looking to find career-driven women. Between coworkers, patients and their family members, I would see attractive women daily. But on this day one was different. A new hire, not tainted by any of the other losers who would try to woo her. She was untouched. She had no idea who I was and I wanted to keep it that way. She sparked something in me that made me want her. Maybe it was the challenge, I don't know. All I knew is that I would have her. I will call her "Lady". "Lady" carried herself in a manner that suggested men should bow before her. Like an amazon goddess, she had class, strength and poise. She walked as if blameless, but from my experience I knew better. She was exactly the type of woman I enjoyed breaking, the ultimate hunt. Her speech was eloquent, her voice melodious. Her skin was the honey to my chocolate and I knew that I would have to overcome some obstacles in order to obtain what it was I wanted from her. I had made up my mind: I would make her want me so badly, that she would forgo logic for the pleasure I would give her. Needless to say, I got her phone number shortly after meeting her and made plans to go to her place in the days to follow.

One reason for my success with women was my belief that none of them were beyond my reach. Remember the P.O.A. theory? No woman or man, if given the proper incentive, is outside of anyone's reach. Believe that. The first time I went over to "Lady's" house she resisted everything I threw at her. This was expected after all, ladies don't give it up on the first night, right? Appearances must be kept and she knew the chase would be boring if she submitted after my initial attempts. Conquering

someone is more enjoyable when they are a worthy adversary.

Time is always on your side when you have a goal in mind and

the resolve necessary to reach it.

    I eventually accomplished my goal in a matter of weeks. It

didn't take the usual empty promises and feelings that I had used

in the past to string in broken women. No, "Lady" was broken

and accepted it. I was a means to her end and I capitalized on

that concept and did not waste time trying to charm her. All I had

to do was be available.

    "Lady's" belief that she was broken and her general idea
that relationships "don't work" placed her in a cage. She thought
that she had given herself freedom by relieving herself of the
constraints of commitment. However, her belief that all
relationships the same and wanting to get away from that actually
limited her, rather than liberated. She had created a cage for her
freedom. Any cage, no matter how big or small, sets rules for you.
If people know you are limited, they can dance around the edge of
your cage getting what they want, while giving you nothing.

<u>Escaping Your Own Cage</u> - Like Houdini, you must learn to escape from your own restraints. This isn't just smoke and mirrors. These cages, though in your minds, have a very real hold on you. It is up to YOU to break that hold.

1) Identify your cage- Not all cages are the same. Just as you take the time to identify the way you love you must also take the time to identify the things preventing you from loving properly. Most of our cages come from one of two things:

a) A negative experience-Typically this has to be something serious enough to cause an aversion to certain behaviors. These behaviors are hard to avoid, so people associate certain behaviors with certain characteristics. For example, at a younger age a woman was molested by a family friend. The family friend was a man who had red hair and freckles. Now whenever approached by a man with these physical characteristics, she is immediately turned off. Think about your behavior and why you continue doing them. If you did your Love history lesson, it should not be hard to isolate the things that potentially build cages around your heart.

b) Learned behavior- This is romantic avoidance taught by defecting certain things. Examples: Not dating certain races, not dating military men, or not dating someone with kids. These things are ingrained in us, and this is how your cage is formed. We become victims of our own programming.

2) Open the door to your cage- Once you figure out what it is that is holding you back from being able to love others, you must consciously focus on not allowing those obstacles to destroy you. For years I believed that relationships were not for me because of who I was in college. Bad Karma and all that. I purposefully avoided people who had the potential to give me something of value. But leaving my cage was not such an easy task. Remember, we are creatures of habit and the cage, though not a practice, has the same connotations as a habit. Make that one change and see how it affects your relationships.

3) Practice Loving free-Go into your relationships with an open mind. Even when released back into the wild after

years of being domesticated, animals will try to hold on to their cages . It is easy to go back to our comfort zones. However, practicing a state of free łLove in which you do not create cages for yourself takes work. Once you liberate yourself its is even harder to stay liberated. Stay persistent.

4) Remove your boundaries-Once you begin living and loving freely, you will not revert back. This is a moment of complete conversion and healing. I used to own two cats, and whenever I had company I had the hardest time putting them back in their cages. When they were young and I was at work they spent most of their time in a cage. But as they grew older they gained more freedom . Now, instead of accepting the cage, they rejected it. Freedom, once experienced, is not easily relinquished. No one who frees themselves from bondage goes back in their cage. If they do, they were never truly free to begin with. So, if you see yourself reverting back to your old ways, STOP. Refocus yourself and go back to step 2.

The most powerful cage is the one your mind constructs. It is hard to overcome your own programming. The bars that lock you in are not made of steel, but of *fear*. Open the door to your own romantic freedom.

8

<u>Catching Your Prey</u>

<u>Four types of a Relationship formation</u>

Cooperation- This occurs when two people get together because they actually enjoy each other. They have weighed their options, the pro's and con's, and they have decided that being together is better than being apart. These relationships tend to occur among two matured individuals. If you are in a relationship like this, then you have a good foundation. This relationship represents a desire for mutual happiness and is often the most successful type.

Obligation- This occurs when one person has some form of pull over another person that results in an unplanned relationship forming. It can be something as simple as, "I didn't want to say no to her because I didn't want to hurt her feelings" or as extreme as, "We're only together for the kids." This type of relationship usually occurs between two immature people. One person lacks the maturity to make a responsible decision, and the other lacks the maturity to recognize that the relationship is a farce. These relationships are more likely to fail.

Temptation- In today's sexually driven world, this form of relationship occurs quite often. How many times have you jumped into a relationship because the sex was good? Many of us (including myself at one point) are guilty of this form of relationship. These relationships can be successful, depending on the individuals involved in the relationship. Any mixture of mature and immature people can be recipe for a temptation driven relationship to form. The success rate is always based on the ability of the couple to establish a foundation other than the temptation that brought them together.

Manipulation- This form of relationship is rarely successful and the reason is because of the intention behind these relationships. For this type, the intentions are typically not to maintain a relationship, but some other means. Example of manipulation based relationships would be : financial dependency, safety and security or any other needs that may be satisfied. These are often the rebound relationships. These relationships serve a specific purpose and once that purpose is satiated the relationship is no longer necessary and can occur with a combination of mature and immature individuals. The only way success occurs with this style of relationship is if the manipulator discovers other reasons for the relationship to continue.

Ex factor- *There are so many different types of relationships that can form. Friendship bonds, romantic, sexual, casual. They originate from a variety of different possible scenarios, but no matter how they form, they connect us to someone else. I've been in countless relationships with a variety of women. Each of us connected in different ways. Some of those connections were not appreciated until after the ties was severed*

I will call her "The lioness". She was a fierce woman with, flowing hair, fair skin, a soft body and hips that beckoned to the hearts of men. I do not know what it was she saw in me. My

potential, my compassion for others, my desire to be loved.
Whatever it was she saw, she liked it, craved it. She spoke of a
greatness in me that I could not foresee. She hungered for me.
That hunger gave motivation for her to provide for my needs.
Whatever it took to keep me around, she would do; mentally,
physically, or emotionally. Whatever I needed she made sure I
had it in abundance.

Things should have been perfect, but I knew that the
entirety of our relationship was built on what she was doing for
me. I did care for her and was happy with her, but in my heart I
knew I could not be what she wanted and that would only result
in her heart breaking. Our relationship was one of obligation. I'm
sure under different circumstances things would have worked
out...but these weren't different circumstances.

A lion peers across the Serengeti, driven by a hunger that
needs to be satiated. Its prey is unaware they have been spotted
and carries on with life as usual. The lion makes its moves,
calculates the obstacles, assesses the state of its quarry and finds
the perfect moment to strike, pouncing before its prey even knows

what hit them.

This sounds like something from National Geographic but the truth is, this is human nature at its core. We are creatures who seek opportunity. We check the scene before making our move. We go for what we want. So what happens when the *what* is a *who*?

Now you are the hunter. You have your sights set on someone you like, someone you need, someone you crave. But that someone is not aware of you or is moving at a pace that you think is too slow. How do you reel them in? How do you get the person you want to notice you? To want you? How do you make the person of your dreams a reality?.

Before discussing the ways, we must first pregame. We need to set the stage for the hunt. First thing you need to know is what it is you want. If you already have an individual in mind, then this part will just be a reference for you. But for those who don't know, figure out *what* it is you are looking for, not *who*. If you are clueless as to what you want, your chances of finding it are better when you keep an open mind and lower restrictions. It is okay to not have an idea of what you want. That is not the same as not having standards. The *what* should be a simple set of words; a husband, a wife, a boyfriend or girlfriend, a friend with benefits or a one night stand. You should always hunt with this in mind- Is this person what I was looking for? Did I achieve my goal? The answer to these questions will tie back into your level of satisfaction with your Lover.

You will now tie in all of the prior lessons that you learned to assess and set a game plan. Understanding how you love and your Love style will teach you the types of people you should look for and avoid. It will also give you a guideline on how you should conduct yourself. This is the center of your web.

Next, remove your flaws (or at least hide them well) prior to engaging your prey. Keep in mind your Love plan and what it is you are looking for the other person. This is the foundational strands of your game plan. Your efforts should be streamlined and focused. I like to be spontaneous and add randomness to a relationship, but even randomness should be something you are in control of. Once you lose sight of who you are, what you are doing or where you want to be, you become the prey you were hunting, and your relationship slips into one where you are reacting rather than moving with conviction. Your original prey gains the power to control your moves.

Make every step count. Flawlessness should be like a tiger blending in with his surroundings. You are the tiger, and the surroundings that you are trying to blend in with is life of your prey. Your presence should feel natural. That is how you get in; - by belonging. Now you can either genuinely fit, or you can become a chameleon and learn how to adaptively blend in. The choice is yours and should reflect your intentions.

You have prepared yourself for the hunt, but where do you begin? The lion can see the gazelle, but how does he bring it down? In the first part of this chapter you assessed yourself. Based on this assessment, your Love plan and the *what* you established you want, you can now begin your approach. If the *what* you are looking for is a husband, look for them in a place where you would be okay with that person being, even after you get married. For instance, if you meet him in a club, that is more than likely where he will be when he is not with you once you are together. If a lion wants to eat a gazelle, he must go where gazelles frequent. A fisherman doesn't go to the desert expecting to find tuna. This should be the same mindset you have when searching for the kind of partner you want. Likewise, looking for a one night stand on a marriage website would be ill advised. Granted you will most likely get a one night stand because sex is one of the four paths to a relationship, but it will definitely bring you unnecessary strife. Stick to your dating diet. Meaning, stay in your lane and focus on what you want.

Along with picking places you would be okay with your partner frequenting, you should search for places that have low levels of competition. If there are more predators than prey in any environment, someone will go hungry. Likewise, if you choose areas where there are others looking for the same thing you are looking for, you will find a shortage in what it is you seek. A prime example of this is church. Statistically, more women go to church than men, with odds of sometimes 10:1. With that being the case, five of those women may be single and looking for a husband. Since there is such a short supply and so many predators vying for the same prize, one of two things will occur. Either one, the guy realizing his situation will grab as much attention as possible (that's what I would do). Or two, whoever is at the top of the food chain is going to eat. Meaning whoever has the most to offer will win. This may not be ideal for all, so instead they should search in areas where there is an abundance and less competition . Proper hunting grounds are essential to ensure your dating survival. Animals are territorial by nature because they instinctually know resources are limited. In the same sense as with tapping into our animal side, we should realize that competition is real and that at any moment there may be others going after the same hunt we are. You have to be at the top of your game.

Essentially dating has two main components: the approach and the close. How you introduce yourself to someone is your approach. Buying a woman a beer, leaving "hey sexy" notes on someone's door, or getting a friend to introduce you are all introductions that initiate the dating sequence. The close is how you actually set up dating. "Will you go out with me?" "I'd like to get into your pants." "Call me sometime." Those are your closers. This lets the person your interested in know you notice them and it establishes the grounds for how you will date each other. Anything that occurs between the approach and the close is filler, aka communication that increases or decreases your chances for a date, which is also important for the close, but not necessary. You can essentially approach and close right after, without any filler, and still get the same result, but only if you know what you're doing. However, most people are not so easily swayed so you have to add a little substance to sweeten the deal.

Dating has evolved over the past few years. Social media has created a new outlet for people to meet. Technology has forever changed the way individuals encounter one another. Someone's in-person dating habits can be COMPLETELY different from how they interact on-line. The internet is a new hunting ground. Most people disclose so much information on social media that figuring them out is not hard at all. However, most on-line interactions don't remain on-line. Thus, do not set expectations about how someone is after an on-line communication alone. Some people gain new found confidence behind a computer screen but in person lack the same courage. We will talk about on-line dating at a later portion of the book.

Since we are talking now about the nature of dating, I'd like to incorporate natural symbols that best represent human traits exhibited while dating. Remember, you must keep in mind all of the things you have discovered about yourself before determining your Love style.

The Lion - aggressive/aggressive - Lions are very interesting creatures. The male lion's mane is almost like its crown. It is a symbol of status. Lion's do not shy away. They see prey that they want and they go after it. Someone who dates with a lion style is no different than an actual lion. They are often brazenly bold with little regard for the possibility of rejection. When they see something they like, they go for it. Straightforward statements like, "You should give me your number," or "We should go out," are normal for lion daters. They are essentially the kind who make dating interesting and are so direct it is entertaining.

The Tiger – passive/aggressive - Tigers wait for the right opportunity before making a move, however, once opportunity presents itself, they attack it with everything they have. They are calculated, ferocious and determined. This style of dating is most closely related to a seductive approach. Tigers isolate their target and study them, draw them in with a false sense of security, and make a move to ensure they get what you want.

The Wolf – passive/passive - Wolves are some of the most interesting animals when it comes to mating habits. They are patient. EXTREMELY PATIENT. A wolf can nip away at an animal and follow it for miles, waiting for it to die before the wolf makes a move. There are people who date this same way. They will be the friend, get to know someone, hang out a few times, exchange numbers, talk on the phone for years before moving to the next level in the relationship. Their staying power is amazing, but they struggle making a romantic relationship happen.

The Spider - aggressive/passive - Spiders work hard in the beginning to capture their prey. The amount of time spent weaving a web is the most important thing that they can do to ensure the success of the hunt. All day, they weave and build and construct intricate webs that capture a multitude of prey. Then they wait. People who date like a Spider work hard to establish a relationship and put themselves in the best possible position for success. They allow suitors to come to them. This is very effective because it gives the "prey" the impression they have control over the relationship. Perspective is king in the world of dating. Manipulation of their lover's perspective gives the Spider reign over their heart. Just wait.

9

Hard Truths

Okay, here comes the part of the book everyone has dreaded. It's not positive, but it's real. Are you ready for it? Here it is...EVERYBODY WILL NOT FIND SOMEONE. This is based on the logistics of the human population male-to-female ratio. The sad truth is that between the difficulty for singles to meet other singles, and the fact that some people are too stubborn to change, not everyone will find someone. However, there is someone out there for everyone. Black, white, fat, skinny, short, tall…there is someone out there who likes what you got. Your task is to showcase what you got and reel 'em in, right? Your job is to make yourself as appealing as you possible.

Love is something you work at, and so are all the traits that make up relationships. Most people are bad at dating from day one, and after a few faux pas, finally get a halfway decent system for love and relationships. But a lot of the time, people blame their failed relationships on the other person: he cheated on me, she didn't trust me, they were this and they were that. Nobody likes to look at their own issues. Before we look outward and learn how to show off our potential, we have to shed that old skin. I will highlight those "wonderful" things that you do that make you unattractive to potential suitors, create roadblocks that keep you from meeting people, and your poisonous traits that make your Lovers run the other way. So here it is....the LIST.

1. *You can't get over your past* - Who cares about what your ex did to you. Obviously whatever formula they used was wrong because they became your ex. Unless the information is pertinent and necessary for the current situation....don't bring it up. Learn to forget about the scars of past Lovers . Don't bring baggage into a new relationship. Think of a relationship as a

weightlifter. He is not strong enough to carry much extra weight initially, so when the relationship is new, it is best to keep things as light as possible. As he keeps lifting, his strength increases. As you grow further away from your past you are able to deal with more. But leave the past in the past.

2. *You're high maintenance or too hard to please* - You want someone to jump through hula hoops to make you happy. Eventually that someone will want to take those hoops and beat you with them. Sometimes you need to chill the heck out. If your lover is working hard to take care of you, appreciate it. No guy wants a chick who is high maintenance. A lot of women confuse high class and high maintenance, but I'm here to clarify it for you. I got you. We will use cars to compare the two. A high class vehicle is a Bugatti Verone: custom paint job foreign made engine with import parts. You can't find it just anywhere; it is one of a kind, a collector's item. A high maintenance engine is like a Chevy Cavalier, the one you had in college that-costs more to keep running than it was worth. Do not make someone question if you are worth the mess you put them through, because often

you're not. Lose the self-inflated value of self, because relationships, like the economy, have reshaped the value of a lot of items on the market. Some items depreciate once you get them off the lot. This goes for guys too. When she makes you dinner, don't complain because it's not as good as your mom's. Too much of that and you'll end up back there. Lower your standards just a tad. Nobody's perfect, including you. In reality people too high of expectations are usually more jacked up than the people they are dating.

3. *You always have to be right* - Nobody likes someone who always has to be right. I was given this title often, but I'm okay with being wrong if someone can show me why I'm wrong. I dealt with a lot of emotional Lovers who wanted to tell me how they feel, but logically could not justify most of their feelings. Having to be right all the time demeans your partner's intelligence. If you like feel this is you, use more tact in your speech toward other when you are expressing your thoughts and know when being right actually matters. Don't correct someone over trivial things. It doesn't matter who chose to go see a

particular movie; the important part is you saw it.

4. *Your horrible in bed*- Contrary to popular belief you may not be as good in bed as you think you are. I will get deeper into this later in the book but think about it like this: sex is like sports. Some people are all-stars who play all over the field, some people are good athletes and play the game well enough people stay interested; some people are benchwarmers and only come in when someone else isn't on their game; others are coaches who want to tell others how to run the play but don't play the game themselves; and there are spectators who don't do anything but watch and speculate and imagine what it would be like to be in the game. Sex is a deal breaker for some, (I have deleted a few numbers for the chick being bad in bed).

5. *You can't commit*- The idea of being tied down freaks you out. Why is that? Is it the connection you fear? Or the fear of loss? Refer to Chapter 1. Understand yourself and be a better Lover. Also Some people can't do this because they are not ready to settle down.

6. *You move too fast*- Moving too fast is not always about

sex. Asking for a title or imposing on someone's privacy too soon can make them withdraw. Trying to get sex too soon can give the impression that is all you care about. Pace yourself, set the cruise control and roll with it.

7. *Too needy*- Are you an emotional parasite that can only survive by sucking the Love and life out of everyone you date? It is draining to have to take care of someone who always needs something. Whether it's physical (things like money, a ride to work, or watching their kids) or emotional (tell me you love me, tell me you're attracted to me, tell me I matter), no one likes a relationship dependent mooch.

8. *Not on the same path in life*-The path I'm referring to is usually one of progression. When people realize you are content with the mediocrity of your life, it can remove all of the sparkle from your relationship. A career minded woman who has dreams of a future and a family is not going to remain with the guy who is 30, lives with his mom and is a gamer (unless he has made a profitable career of it) whose idea of date night is standing in line waiting for the new Madden to release at midnight. He will be

dismissed. A guy who is in the position to establish himself as a leader at work and will want to bring a woman of equal caliber around his coworkers (it's nice when you can brag on your lady), and who is secure in himself will want a woman who can match his talents and accomplishments.

9.*Kids*- There are multiple reasons for this. As a matter of fact, I myself struggled with this one. Anytime kids come into play in dating it makes everything more complicated. The complexities can be one of any number of variables. As much as you would like to think the adults have the power, let that little one start to dislike your partner. If it comes down to choosing, usually you will be gone. There is the possibility of a co-parent who hopefully will understand your role in their kid's life. Nobody wants baby momma drama. It's distasteful and immature, but it's real. There is the possibility that your partner isn't good with kids. Not to say they can't learn, but it can make dating rough. Or maybe the person you are dating is a bad parent and you can't deal. Then of course there's always the "I don't really want kids" scenario that usually ends at the mention of little people. So yeah...kids are complex. Really evaluate before getting involved with someone with kids.

10.*Money issues*- In today's economy that can be anyone. Who is to say someone isn't just down on their luck. But down on your luck usually has a time limit. A man being able to provide is almost as much of a requirement as having a Y chromosome. Learn the difference between being financially smart and cheap. Women who always want to spend money (especially someone else's) will usually have problems keeping a lover, or will at least be the cause of a lot of arguments. You should view love as a business deal. Would you merge with a company that is losing money if you are profiting? There are no buyouts in love, so your partner's financial problems become yours. I will get into this more in the next chapter.

11.*Too down for the homies*- Guys or girls, if your relationship always consists of doing things with your friends, it is not a relationship. Learn to separate from the pack. You should not spend all of your time with the girls or the guys, but instead should dedicate time to your significant other. Also, keep your friends out of all your business. You never know who is rooting for you to fail so they can swoop in and get what you have.

12. *You have no life, aka you're boring* -You never want to go out. You never want to do anything new. You're a hermit, and nobody likes a hermit. There is a difference between liking to do things at home and being a hermit. If all you do is go to work and come home and eat and have sex, you are a victim of routine relationships. If you can't say that in the last three months you did anything new or different, you may be the boring one.

13. *You're a runner, meaning, you give up too easy*-The first sign of any trouble, you're gone. Now for some situations this is wise. If your partner exhibits an angry outburst in public or if they shows early signs of possible infidelity, then leave. But if you run because they like football and your ex ignored you during football season, or because they likes to spend time with their mother once a month (which does not constitute a momma's boy), then you need to ease your jets and give it a chance. And fellas, just because she asks your future plans does not mean that she intends to be in them. Your answers may give her cause to hit the

eject button.

14.*You're not good enough/self-esteem issues*- "Woe is me. I've been cheated on. Waaaaahhh! I just wish someone would love me. Waaaaaah!" Stop. No one likes a victim or an emotional doormat. You think you're such an awful person, no one will ever love you and you're not that special. Take stuff at face value. You have had some bad relationships, so has everyone else. Don't ruin the next one because you went into it as a negative Nancy.

15.*Forcing change or being afraid of it*- Trying to change someone will make them resent you. Now, changing who someone is and changing their habits are not the same. Changing a habit is like getting someone to put down the toilet seat or try a new diet. Changing who someone is would be asking a comic fan to throw away all his comics because they are for kids (ladies comics are a culture beyond what you perceive, just like those romance novels you read only with epic fight scenes and super powers) or making someone change their beliefs to fit yours. That resentment will poison your relationship. Also, being rigid to change will make someone cold to you. Relationships are about compromise. If you are a statue on everything that matters to them, you will stop mattering to them. Remember, the only constant is change.

16.*Family*- Differences in family make up and expectations have an effect on how you choose a mate. Some people make dating decisions based on the approval of mommy or daddy and some people are too close to their parents to the point where you wonder who is dating who. Momma's boys and daddy's girls can be hard to grow with. Also, unresolved parental issues can lead to poor dating choices. A lot of guys prey on girls with daddy issues. Many women learn to manipulate men who had dependent relationships with their mothers and used that as a means to control them, becoming a pseudo-mom. Don't be one of them. A good practice early in your dating relationship with anyone is to gauge the relationship they have with their family.

17.*You don't get out*- Now we live in a world where meeting new people can be as simple as a click of a mouse. However, you still have to get out eventually. There were periods of my life where I worked so much that dating wasn't feasible. If I did date, it would have been with someone at the workplace, which is usually disastrous. If you want to meet new people I got a crazy idea for you. Go someplace new. New places hold new people and new experiences. If you go to the same coffee shop expect to see the same people.

18. *You don't really want to date, you just think you do-* There are people who date because their friends are dating, because their "getting up in years", or because it's just the right thing to do. This is always wrong. First, you have to decide if you have the desire to deal with another person romantically, because on top of having to contribute to the good, you also have to put up with the bad. Relationships take work, and some people want to stay unemployed. Second, you need to decide if you have the capacity to give another human being the love they would need. Nothing sucks harder than being involved with someone who is incapable of loving you. It's not that they are bad or anything. Some people are either burnt out by life, coping with other situations, or just lack the time to be the person you need. If you can't commit, be fair and walk away

So, are you someone people want? Are you the dream guy? Are you wife material? Most people believe they are of greater quality than they really are. And everyone wants someone who is probably better off than they are nowadays.

10

<u>The Love Business</u>

What if I told you that every relationship, every interaction, every intimate moment, extended or otherwise was no different than a business deal? This concept is not as cold as it may initially appear. I use this metaphor to make understanding certain aspects of relationships a little easier. You are now the CEO of LUVME, inc. You have been looking to expand your business into new markets and decided a joint venture is a step you are ready to make. Let's break down the components you will need to consider before taking your business to the next level. Beyond being the CEO, see yourself as the business. All of its components and operations, and everything that happens to it is a reflection of what happens to you.

The first step for your company, LUVME, inc, is to establish a business plan. Every business, whether its is a small town diner or a large multinational corporation, has a plan. Some are long and drawn out with hundreds of pages and diagrams and complicated terms. Others are much simpler, having a simple outline of business and how it is to be conducted. This is your Love plan and it will shape the decisions you make in regards to your love life.

For this, you need to have an idea of where you want to go, not so much how you want to get there. What you want to do, and not how you are going to do it. What you expect from dating, and what your end goal will be. If you don't establish your own plan then you end up falling victim to somebody else's. How often have you or someone you know been in a relationship and then all of the sudden your Lover's interests become your interests? You become dissolved as a lesser party in the relationship. An established Love plan will allow you to retain a sense of self while engaging other parties. This should be a guide and not a strict rule. For example, looking for a serious relationship does not mean don't casually date. Most people can't determine if you are someone they will take seriously until they getting to know you. Your Love plan should be like an executive summary, or a brief synopsis of what you envision your love life to be. It should not include expectations of others, only expectations of yourself and goals you want to meet. You cannot say, "I expect to meet a guy with an income of $75,000 annually," and then set that as your standard for dating. Your plan should be as follows:

*Meet someone

*Date for X number of years

*Get married

*Have kids after X number of years

*Have X number of kids

Your Love/business plan should, at minimum, have an END GOAL that starts from the point you are at currently. However, your plan does not have to be the same all the time. Just as businesses evolve, your Love plan can change whenever you see the need. As life hits us, our plans change. So do our desires for love and relationships. It would make sense for a flexible plan to be in place to account for changes you may experience in life that spill over into your love life. I would advise keeping the same plan for a considerable amount of time to determine if that plan is right for you. Rapidly changing your plan does not allow you to determine success or failure, so give it a chance before you change. Marriage may sound good but if you are working two jobs, meeting someone new may be hard. Allow yourself a few casual encounters until your life can get back to the original plan.

We have a plan. What's next? It is time to conduct business. The important part of this is selecting someone who aligns with your ENDGOAL. This person needs to fall in line with your Love plan. If you and your partner are not on the same frequency, one of two things will happen: Either one person's Love plan will succeed while the others is eclipsed or, neither of your Love plans will come into fruition. Two companies that plan to do short-term business with one another do not need a stringent set of rules for their interactions. Simple transactions that do not require in-depth detail will suffice . Companies that are looking for a long term partnership or potential merger pay closer attention to the details the others may have left out. Relationships are no different. If your Love plan does not have any serious components, then there is no need for a bunch of stress. Call when you want to see them. Don't meet the family. Have fun. However, with more serious goals like marriage or children, you want to look into the other company's history to determine if there will be a viable future.

Finding someone whose Love plan is similar to yours will make things so much smoother. If someone's love plan differs from yours that does not mean you can't be with them. However, your expectations should not be that high. For example, Pepsi is a top beverage production and distribution company and Susie has a lemonade stand on 5th and Monroe. If Pepsi comes to Susie with a joint venture proposal, Pepsi should not be upset with Susie if she can't match Pepsi's contribution. So that guy or girl you met at the bar last night who said they weren't looking for anything serious, just a good time, and they give you their number. Do not be upset if you don't get that official title a few months down the road (or not at all). They were just following their plan. Even if you try to switch them over to your plan it will probably backfire and you will get the shoulder shrug, a look of pity and those three words, "It's just business" before ending up back at the drawing board to reevaluate your plan.

Ex Factor- *I was 24 and I was a jerk. Not for the sake of being a jerk, I was just focused on my business at the time. I had a music management company that required a lot of my time. On top of working full time and other responsibilities, love was just not on my plate of things to do. Yet sometimes, we don't have to search for it to come looking for us. Through a mutual acquaintance, I met "Honey", a bronze skinned full-figured woman who smiled constantly. It drove me insane how happy she was all the time. Not in a good way. I felt like she was a fan more than a lover.*

She and I started dating because she manipulated her way into my life. I didn't find this out until later on though. I made it obvious what I needed was support, support in building my dream and achieving those life goals I had deemed important. So that's what she became. Everything I wanted to do, she wanted to do. She was passionate about my passions and I loved and hated that at the same time. It sounds confusing but I felt like her life revolved around me. She was the moon orbiting my existence and she was beginning to push me away.

The issues came when she wanted more from our arrangement than I had been giving. I had stated early on that I had no interest in ANYTHING that would distract from my goals, especially not a relationship. Her whole reasoning for her support was to eventually gain the title of being mine. When it became clear that my mind was made up, the relationship ended, along with her support. We had two different plans entirely and it was best we separate then fail miserably trying to achieve both.

LOVEME, inc. has a plan to establish a long-term serious relationship with moderate to excessive time spent adjoining the two entities. Profit margins would be split 50/50 with room for adjustments as necessary. The plan should take no less than six months of negotiations and no more than one-and-a-half years before establishing a deal. Both partners agree to contribute 50% of their equity and investments into making the deal work. The end goal is a company merger with unification of all assets and properties.

That's was a little wordy. Here's a simpler version of the same thing...

Translation: you want a serious relationship. One in which you spend a little more time together, less than a live in mate but more than long distance. You want a 50/50 relationship where you do for each other, but understand that there may be times where someone has to carry more. You want to be dating at least six months before getting serious, but no longer than a year and a half. You want someone who is just as committed to making this deal work as you and who shares the same desired goal of marriage.

This can also be done with a significant other to gauge where you both see the relationship going and to evaluate where you are as a couple. Fortify your love life and establish confidence by having a game plan in life and love. Chance favors the prepared mind. As a lover you want to be a Fortune 500 company. Make loving you, an enriching experience, and have a plan as to how you will love and be loved.

Ex Factor- *She will be known as "The Neighbor". I was 23 years old, single and had just relocated to an apartment not far from downtown to be closer to my new job. This job was so important to me at the time that I couldn't focus on much of anything else. I would wake up, go to work, come home, eat and go to sleep. Truth be told I didn't WANT anything, with anyone. I was enjoying my solitude. I did what I wanted and I was saving money because I didn't have to worry about taking care of anyone else. I answered to no one. But I still had a desire for the occasional intimate encounter. The issue was getting what I wanted without having to deal with any other obligations.*

I would call up the occasional evening companion to help me burn some time as well as some energy. But each woman that I invited to my place became fixated on some ill placed hope that there would be more between us. That wasn't happening. Nothing personal. Just a place in my life where relationships did not matter, and neither did they.

I was washing clothes one night in the laundry room wearing shorts and a t-shirt. The laundry room was located right below my apartment, so I would often just sit down there and wait for my clothes to finish. It was close to midnight and I was alone, until she walked in. "The Neighbor" was a full-figured woman with a lighter complexion and plain features. She lived on the 10th floor of our building, which would explain why I hadn't seen her prior to this night. She had her hair pulled back in a ponytail and was wearing sweatpants and a sleeveless shirt. Probably because her clothes were still washing. After some brief conversation we realized that we both wanted the same thing. NOTHING. No obligations, no expectations and no commitments. Just a moment of pleasure to hold us over until the next time the urge hit us again.

She would come to my place, I would play video games after we were done and she would leave. I would go to her place, she would watch True Blood, and I slept. We were giving each other nothing. But at this point in our lives, that was all we

needed.

11

<u>The Love Brand</u>

*<u>**Love Brand-**</u> characteristics that add or subtract value from your Love as perceived by others.*

      The next thing you need to do as CEO of LUVME, inc. is to establish how viable the product you have is to sell and the potential you have to attract buyers. Your product, of course, is YOU. Take an honest look at yourself. Would you date you? What would it take to make yourself irresistible to others? Like any product that you want people to buy, you must invest in making a brand that is top notch. This means offering the best of yourself and being at your best. This does not necessarily mean lose 50 lbs. because not every guy wants a runway model and not every woman wants a bodybuilder. Remember, you're presenting YOUR product, not trying to imitate someone else's.

A brand is anything that distinguishes a business or entity from others of the same caliber. Your brand can be your image, your reputation, your product offering, features, or it can be all of these things. Example:

*The Nike sign is a part of its brand.

*The design of Apple phones is a part of its brand.

* How the PlayStation Network is free compared to the Xbox Live network, which is a distinct product offering that their customers look for.

In regards to your Love brand, it should be your goal as well and to distinguish yourself as unique from others. Create an image of yourself that is true to your best characteristics. Some statements I have heard repeatedly are things like, "All men are the same," or "All women are crazy." Although these statements do harm by grouping all in the same box, they also create opportunities to make your brand stand-out. A simple way to think about it is if every restaurant on the boardwalk serves hamburgers and then suddenly here you come with cheeseburgers, you have set yourself apart as different and with more to offer.

Image is everything, but only in the sense of presentation when it comes to dating. It is YOUR job to present the best image possible. It is not shallow to use appearance as a criteria for determining who to date. It is shallow to make it the ONLY criteria. You must control your image and understand what the image of others says about them. A person's Love brand speaks volumes. Their brand is a representation of how they love and want to be loved. Do not take lightly the things that someone's brand says about them.

Shaping your Brand: Brands evolve, grow and mature just as people do. As they experience different things, such as cultural changes or shifts in customer needs, companies reshape their brand in order to be better received by potential customers. In the same way your Love brand should have the same fluidity. The guy who was a nerd back in high school that nobody gave the time of day re-emerges as a handsome hunk with women fawning over him constantly. The girl from college who was 280 lbs. but after a dedicated regimen of diet and exercise slimmed down to a sexy frame that makes all the boys drool. These people recognized there was reason for things not going the way they wanted, so they made a change. Brands change the customer's perception of companies and it can change other people's perception of you. They can either ENHANCE it or DIMINISH it. The effect your Love brand has on your perception is completely up to you.

Ex Factor- *Sometimes what we "know" can distract from how we feel. Past wrongs distract from current feelings. This is especially true for those who put logic over emotion. That was me. It had its own taste of irony. Me having issues with someone else's past knowing how extreme and extensive my own was. But that is how we are, right? Holding others accountable to standards we don't measure for ourselves.*

I was 22 years old waiting tables at a restaurant when I met her. She actually came right up to me and asked for my number which is not something a lot of women feel confident enough to do. But she had a presence unlike other women. I shall call her "Fuego". The desire that burned within her for me was like an inferno. She was an older woman from the island of Puerto Rico. Her hair was died a crimson red that went well with her golden brown complexion. I can very well say she was one of the most passionate lovers I ever had. We went out for a time, enjoying each other's company. We connected in every way. Things were good, really good. We were almost to the point of "getting serious" when she decided to relay a piece of personal truth.

She had made some decisions in her past that caused me to doubt our potential future. At a younger age she participated in some illegal activities that she claimed were behind her. I believed her, but as we continued on I realized I couldn't get over her past. Although she had shown me something different, her past created a long shadow that impacted my view of her. I was honest with her and she accepted that. One of the hardest and easiest breakups I ever had.

We are drawn to the things we like, but if you can not show the parts of you that someone will like, how can they be drawn to you? Command their focus. If you don't want to attract someone based on physical attributes then you need to make sure whatever it is that you want to use to pull them in is on point. Brands work best if they pull attention to certain aspects. If your selling point is in your personality, you must present that in a way where they will focus on your personality and nothing else. Create the scene that will bring people to your store front. Invest in yourself. The items that companies want you to focus on in a store are typically right there in the front, as soon as you walk in. Put it out there for people to see. You should WANT people to notice the good things about you.

Your physical appearance (or your image) is just one aspect of your Love brand, you also have your reputation (what people know/believe about you) and what you bring to the table (brand features). Learn how to dress in a way that compliments your natural characteristics. Get a gym membership (gyms are actually a great hunting ground for some singles). Spend a little bit more time on your hair. Make sure your shave is flawless. Your image has definite features that are open to interpretation.

To control the physical aspects of your appearance, what you really want to do is control the interpretation. If you have a man and you put jeans and a t-shirt on him he presents an image. The same man wearing gym attire gives a different image. Yet the same man in a custom made suit and tie gives off another. His physical appearance is unchanged, yet the perception of him, the interpretation of his Love brand, has. The clothes don't maketh the man but, it can shapeth how he (or she) is perceived. A lot of factors go into the physical interpretation. Our sight is the first thing that sends a signal to the brain to be interested in someone. Literally anything the eye can see can be attributed to your Love brand The eyes are said to be the doorway to the soul. If you are going to enter someone's soul, make sure you are at your best.

Your reputation is a fragile thing in terms of relationships. All it takes is ONE bad experience to tarnish your Love brand Cheat once and you're labeled a cheater. Lie and you're a liar. All it takes is for one bad situation to change someone's perception of you. This stays with you. Why, you may ask? Because we, as people often find ourselves identifying with how other people see us. However, I'm here to tell you that your reputation does not have to be permanent. Businesses often engage customers to hear about how the customer believes they are doing. All businesses love hearing good news but the great businesses love hearing the bad. When you know what you are doing wrong, you get an opportunity to fix it. Acceptance of mistakes you have made gives you a chance to do better with someone else.

Your Love brand is an identifier. Your Love brand has elements about it that are specific to you, features that define your dating ability. Your qualities that make you special. Spending time to focus on these elements is crucial.

This is your research and development phase. Any company, before they release a product, does an extensive amount of research to make sure it is ready to be released. Companies will even go as far as to beta test a product (allowing a select few people to test out the product before it is available publicly. All of these things are meant to bring out the best aspects of your product. In the case of your Love brand, this means learning how it operates and how to best reach the individuals you seek to have a relationship with. If you are still understanding your love brand, then this is the perfect time for your beta test.

Beta Testing Your Love brand:

1) *Know the best qualities of your Love brand and focus on them.* One of the "features" you want people to focus on in dating is your sense of humor. If you feel it is your most winning trait, make it a focal point when someone looks at you.

2) *Highlight those qualities in scenarios that require dating acceptance.* The next time you go out or the next time you're on a date, make them laugh whenever the opportunity presents itself.

3) *Ask questions.* This is important. Ask your lover about what you're best and worst traits are. If you're response is good, then you know you have put yourself in the position to move forward. However, most people are afraid to do this because they fear honest rejection. Not everything you do is going to be everyone's cup of tea. This just allows you to work on what you need to work on in order to get who you want.

4) *Reshape your brand if necessary.* When things don't go

the way we want, its is okay. We can build upon what we learn and start anew. It is important to learn from a beta test. Just because you call it a "beta test" does not mean it cannot be the foundation of your final product. If it's not broke, don't fix it. Nevertheless, if you learn that you are in need of some adjustments, take them seriously. Be appreciative of the lesson you learned instead of upset that someone doesn't want you. Not everyone will. But someone will.

Apple and Samsung both sell top quality phones, however, Apple's presentation begins long before you ever get a phone. The stores have a modern look, the employees look intelligent, the box your device comes in is clean, and then the device itself is sleek and smooth. This creates an experience for the consumer that makes them feel like they are getting a higher grade device. The same should happen when people meet you. They should feel that dating you is an experience unlike any other. Be top notch....not bottom shelf.

12

The Dating Market

Are the conditions right? Is your location ideal for you to achieve all the goals of your Love plan? You need to assess your market or your dating environment. In the marketing mix, this is known as placement. Is the area that you're in a suitable dating environment? If you live in a hustling city where everyone is in a rush and no one takes the time to talk, how do you create the opportunity to even obtain a date? Once you have determined your Love style and have an understanding of your Love history you can properly gauge the places that would best suit your dating style. For example, if you are a physical Lover and your Love DNA makes you want an exciting relationships, the library may not be the best place to go cruising for dates. Where you try to date also is a reflection of your Love brand If you go to dive bars to meet guys, the guys in there have a perception of the type of women in there. Do not be surprised if your brand is misrepresented due to your choice of Love market

Ex Factor- *I was in another state for an educational expo. I had told myself that while away I would attempt to have some pleasure while conducting business. The expo was pertaining to medical professionals and being that I was a black male at a predominantly white event, there were not many people in my market for me to choose from if I wanted a black woman. I'm all for interracial relationships and have engaged in many myself, but at this point in my life I was infatuated with dark skinned black women.*

I was exploring the hotel trying to find where everything was located when I saw a woman in the lobby downstairs. I will call her "the Doctor". She immediately noticed me as well. A slim figured woman of the chocolate variety. Apparently she had the same idea as me because she approached me and started a conversation that I knew was based solely on the fact that we were of a similar demographic. The market was vast with not much to choose from for either of us. So the decision was made easy by the limited options. An hour later we were making the trip up to my room. I didn't have to even put in the work. The market just had favorable conditions.

Location Location Location- Has anyone ever told you that the reason you can't find love is because you are "looking in all the wrong places." There is definitely some truth to that. Certain areas breed specific love types. You can find a variety of lovers in any particular area. However, like certain businesses, the location may be ideal for some types and not so ideal for others. Don't be afraid to change your scene. I would highly suggest taking some time to go to places you don't normally go. How else are you going to meet people that you wouldn't normally meet? Try a new restaurant, go to the "other mall", travel to a neighboring city and check out the night life. The more markets you are aware of the more options you give yourself. If all you do is go to work and go home, guess how many markets you have to choose from? Two. And one of those is probably slim on pickings.

Choosing a dating market should not be random. You have a Love style and a Love plan, so let these guide your decisions. Do you want some adventure in your life and want to meet someone who's is into the same? Then do something exciting, like rock climbing or kayaking. Do you want something that moves at a slower pace? Try the museums or some good book stores. Pick a market that suits you and begin your search there.

Market Saturation - If you don't put yourself out there, how can you expect anyone to notice you? A company wishing to capitalize on a market must be present within that specific market. In the same sense, if you wish to find love you must be willing to venture into new markets. Staying inside watching Netflix does not promote your Love brand Market selection can be difficult because most people hear the places they are supposed to look from the suggestions of others and don't actually plan what is best for them based on HOW they love. The environment you choose to share your love should be one that coincides with your Love plan, enhances or fits in with your Love brand, and caters to your Love style These three factors are **Essential** to establishing a strong game plan for love and relationships.

Your Love plan- States what you are looking for or where you are trying to be.

Your Love brand- Determines what people perceive about you and how you are represented.

Your Love style- Are the characteristics exhibited by you in romantic situations.

Businesses sometimes have the dilemma of trying to select a location that is not already oversaturated. In selecting your market you have to make sure it is one that is not already "occupied". An excellent example that I use a lot is the church. Most women in church want a man that is also involved in church. However, the majority of churches have a gender ratio of about 5:1. If you have five guys and 25 women all within the same dating range (lets use the ages of 20-35) Out of those five guys, probably three of them are married, leaving two. That leaves 25 women to two AVAILABLE men. See what I mean by over-saturation? This also applies in the reverse. When you have too many options it is hard to determine which Love brand is the best for you and your Love plan Find a market that has the balance you need to make the selection process as easy as possible.

Timing- Sometimes the location may be ideal but the timing may be wrong. Timing is important. In a business setting companies will push back products, delay releases and more to make sure that the timing is optimal to put their best foot forward.

Look at movie releases. Some movies will push back their release so as not to compete with other movies and to ensure their own success. The timing is key. What you need to know is, 1) if the time is right for you, and 2) if the time right is for the situation. Your timing leaves an impression upon your Love brand as well.

Your Timing- Should always be based off of your Love plan, your Love style and your level of readiness. You may have a plan and understand your style but if you are fresh out of a breakup you need to reassess your market before jumping back in the fray. Many people mess up a potentially good thing not because the other person wasn't right, but because the timing was wrong. Sometimes the wait really is worth it.

Situational Timing- Is based on the situation. This is determined by the market you are in and your Love style For example, say you walk in to a restaurant and see a woman sitting alone. You consider yourself an intellectual Lover and know that winning her over with conversation plays to your strengths. However, you see she appears to be studying for an exam as she has papers and school books all over her table. Some witty conversation with a handsome stranger may be what she needs to get her mind a break from bio-chemistry. But chances are she needs to focus and if done incorrectly you could not only ruin ANY chance of romancing her, you will also make yourself look like a jerk. Timing is everything.

The Online Marketplace - There is a serious taboo associated with online dating. It is new, and because of this most people are wary of it. Online dating bears a lot of the same risks and rewards as traditional dating. The internet becomes your "location" with your reach being far more vast than going to the mall or a bar to meet someone. Online dating is great for tailoring your Love brand to be what you would like it to be. However, there is a lot of room to "hide" who you are online. Be wary of online appearances. There are some things that are obvious like fake pictures, or claiming to have jobs that don't match the finances rendered. But some people have found ways to totally recreate themselves online. As with any market you want to make sure that it is right for you. Do your research. Don't think that because it's a different avenue that the rules are different. Stay true to your Love plan It applies even in the digital world.

Your Love market is the realm within which you will be operating. Knowing the rules of the market you are in and how they work with or work against your Love plan, brand and style are crucial to your romantic success. Remember, it is hard to change who you are. But changing the scene (changing your market) is almost as easy as changing socks. Don't be afraid to step out of the box.

13

Stockholders, Stakeholders, and Placeholders

You have established a Love brand and you have found the right market, but before you go all the way in on your new dating enterprise you need to determine the value of your stock. What is your love worth? We often think about the qualities we want in a significant other while overlooking what it is we bring to the table. All of the criteria for success may be in place but our łLove brand may not have passed the initial testing phase. Just like the stock market, value is determined by supply-and-demand and market conditions. We have already established how to evaluate your market. Supply is easily determined as you are but one. So the item you control that increases or decreases your value is demand.

A lot of people either under or over value their love. Things like "I'm a good woman I deserve a good man," "I want a queen," or "Nobody would want to be with someone like me,"are said recklessly without the consideration of what it is you actually deserve. Are you worthy of that perfect guy or girl that you often fantasize about coming into your life? Or have you been handed the just desserts of years of laziness in building the value of your loves stock? One of the biggest factors in determining how products are priced is the perceived value or benefit they offer. Why can you purchase a laptop for $300 while a cellphone can go for $1,000 after tax? Because the demand for phones is higher. Why is the demand higher? Because the PERCEIVED value is higher. Perceived value is set by the audience. A phone can do all that a laptop can do and more, so of course if given the choice you would go for the phone. What does that mean? It means it doesn't matter what you KNOW about you, what matters is what you SHOW about you. People determine our value before they ever sample us. However, the experience of us is what locks them in or sends them running. Every product or service offers certain features. For you, these would be the characteristics in loving you that make it a good or bad experience. In business there is a term known as CONSIDERATION. It is not the same as the consideration we think of but instead refers to both parties exchanging something of VALUE in a business transaction. In most business situations this is the exchange a good for money exchange. The phone is what you want while the money is what Verizon wants. Consideration occurs in all relationships. This is where we weigh the options and make a list of pros and cons. It is in direct relation with the perceived value that you give to someone. If you want just sex, you may not think it is worth it to spend $300 on dinner. Getting what you want, whether it is a one night stand or a lifetime partner must come from the other party seeing your value. If you have been in a long relationship and want to take it to the next level but the other person doesn't, it may be because they do not think they would be getting a fair deal. Remember, consideration involves both parties exchanging something of value. So if they don't feel you're matching their contribution, they will be less likely to take the deal.

Johnny loves Susie

With all of his heart,

But she doesn't work

So it makes things real hard.

Susie loves Johnny

With all of her heart,

She wants to be married

Til death do they part.

Johnny works double

To cover the bill,

This relationship

Has gone over the hill.

Susie lays home and watches TV

Of shows about weddings

And brides to be.

Johnny starts to doubt

If he wants to commit,

To be quite honest

He's sick of her shit.

Susie thinks Johnny's

A heck of a man,

And wonders if marriage

Is part of his plan.

Johnny loves Susie

But she'll never change,

He knows if they marry

She'll just stay the same.

Susie loves Johnny

She's living the dream,

Not knowing that things

Aren't as good as they seem.

Johnny left Susie

Without saying why,

With a heart torn to pieces

And tears in her eye.

Susie hates Johnny

For these feelings she felt

Without realizing the problem

Had started with self.

You have to have something to offer, but it has to be of value to the person you are with. Not all women want a man who is "in touch with his feminine side" and not all men want a woman who can cook. What you bring to the table (your product offering) must cater to your target demographic. Being good in bed and trying to get a church girl is a backwards strategy. That's not to say it wouldn't work, but it's bad form to work against yourself.

Stakeholders in business are the people who stand to benefit from that business. Anyone impacted by the businesses activities is a stakeholder. This includes the president of the company, the employees, volunteers, family members, and customers. In a relationship the stakeholders are anyone who stands the chance being in a relationship with you. Ideally you want to minimize the amount of stakeholders present in any łLove situation. Occasionally you will have situations like children or disabled family members or pets who come packaged with your significant other. Understand that the more people involved the more important it is to maintain value. When a business has a product that starts to lose its value they either fix it or stop selling it. If these people came attached to your Lover, then when your value starts to diminish you will be dropped. It is not that you are not important, but they have circumstances that require you to perform at a certain level. If you can't meet their requirement then it is best for both parties to cease business.

Placeholders are people who occupy your time but serve no purpose in your Love plan. Know this: IF YOU ALLOW SOMEONE TO OCCUPY YOUR TIME, THEY ARE DECREASING YOUR VALUE. Your time has value. If you are wasting it with someone who is only a placeholder you are ultimately lowering your value. Learn the difference between appreciators and depreciators. When someone significant recognized your value, they will want to preserve it.

Ex Factor- *I will call her "No Strings". She was a college senior at a neighboring university who I had met online. She had shown interest in me coming over to spend some time with her so when the opportunity arose, I did. She was a taller woman, which in the past had never been an issue although I preferred women who I could physically do "more" with. When I arrived she seemed to have very little interest in my presence. She put something on the TV and watched it. She didn't really talk much, which was weird since it was her idea that I come over. She ended up telling me she had a boyfriend, which didn't bother me because her boyfriend didn't mean anything to me.*

We continued to sit there in a semi-silence before she announced, "I'm going to my bedroom, want to come?" The first night resulted in physical intimacy and when it ended she asked me to leave. This worked fine for me because things usually were weird the morning after.

I left with everything I came with. No call to make sure I got home safe, no good morning text the next day. Just...nothing. We continued this relationship with no connection off-and-on for about a year. I called her, she came and left, and vice versa. Neither of us staying to give comfort to the other, to cuddle, to kiss. I'm sure out of the two of us I was the most affectionate, and that is not saying much. Frankly, we didn't even like each other that much. We were just satisfying a temporary need. I'm not sure if her boyfriend was not around or was bad in bed but the frequency with which we were together made me question his role in her life. But it didn't matter because I played no role, we were just taking up space, wasting each other's time. For what, I' was not sure. This went on for a while before I just stopped taking her calls. I had more important things to do.

There is one surefire way to ensure a rise in your perceived value, and that is a rise in stock. Find the things that you don't like about yourself and work to change or remove what you have the power to change. This will make you feel better about yourself and raise your confidence. If there is one thing I know to be true, it is that the lack of confidence is unattractive to everyone. Feel good about you. Control your value by

controlling it perception. Understand what you have to offer and

don't offer it to just anyone. Remember, your value depends on it.

14

The Playbook

This chapter is intended solely for those who are either only interested in romantic conquest or need to know how to recognize the wiles of someone trying to manipulate them. I will give two sides to every point I make in this chapter. If we are discussing the playbook then we will see the player side as offense and the anti-player side as defense. X's and O's. This is going to be a straight forward play-by-play approach on romantic conquest.

The Approach- Every encounter has an approach and a close. When being a player the goal is to get as much as possible while giving very little information about yourself or your intentions. Being a good player means being a great conversationalist. I would often prepare three or more items of conversation that could be built upon if need be. Most women love to talk, so a man who can carry intelligent conversation and speak eloquently enough is usually in the winners category(for men, the amount you can talk is not as important as their knowledge of subject matter). You must also be well versed on a number of subjects and be able to steer conversation in a direction that enhances your chances of looking good. For you, the approach is all about killing that first impression and creating enough intrigue about yourself that your subject will want to know more. Once you have created the necessary environment, your next goal is to leave the situation with something; an email, a phone number, a Facebook, some form of contact. In order to ensure the most success I suggest the form of communication that gives the least amount of risk. Nowadays it is easier to add someone on Facebook and get the phone number later. Asking for someone's number can cause them to pull away from any image you have created if done improperly. So be selective in your wording.

Defense- For every answer you give get one in return. Do not allow doubt to be clouded by the mystery of this would-be Lover. What he or she wants is for you to get lost in the details. You having a high level of awareness works against their agenda, which is the element of surprise. It is okay to communicate with someone you perceive to be a player. How you flip the script is by maintaining control. So instead of giving them your number, ask for theirs. An ego is a valuable thing for someone aspiring to be a "player", so in order to keep theirs intact they will accept whatever you throw their way. Control the pace and run your race.

Time Together- Being a player often means dividing your time with more than one man or woman. IT IS A FULL-TIME JOB. This is what turns most people off from wanting to live this lifestyle. It can sometimes require MORE work than an actual relationship. However, if you are engaging in polygamist like activities, it is probably not for the abundance of love but for the thrill that is experienced from it. Timing is everything and you must be in total control of your time and the time of those you pursue. You must always be aware of where your conquests are at all times. Even if they are not with you, they could see you, or run into you at the store, or call you at inopportune times. Know how to control this. Establish a relationship with one where he or she believes that they can't reach you by phone. Another that you hate text messaging, Another that you "don't do social media" and only have a page for family purposes. There are a multitude of ways to keep someone out of the loop in regards to how you are spending your time. Create a schedule and keep to it.

Defense-Most "players" hate surprises. As in surprise visits, or surprise phone calls, etc. You must dictate how large your presence will be and not allow yourself to be penciled in to someone else's time table. You have to do this in a way that does not make you appear clingy. You should be selective about when to do this. A lot of people who are "players" are intelligent and experienced at "the game", so if they catch on to what you are trying to do, then the suitor will have an opportunity to adjust. Intentional tardiness can also help to control your presence, however if it becomes excessive you can expect to be written off. Make them schedule around you. Not the other way around.

Perception-Your reputation must be kept under control. That means that every man or woman you engage must know essentially nothing about any other romantic activities you may have going on. Do not let your ego destroy what it is that you are trying to accomplish. If you allow it to slip out that you are loving more than one person at a time, it can easily backfire on you. It does not benefit you to tell others about your conquests unless those conquests are no longer in play. Also, make sure that you can control all the moving pieces you are engaged with. You must come off as someone who has it all together. If you look like you are constantly running, it takes away from the charm of being dating you. Control what people see about you.

Defense- Be wary of people who have to appear perfect. This does not appear only to "players" but this is just good general knowledge. If who you are dating appears to be perfect, there is probably something going on. To poke a hole in this, become involved with their "circle." This is family, friends, coworkers, or someone who knows them well enough to know their habits and trends. Most of the time a "player" will want to keep you at a safe distance so they can better control the information that you are able to take in from them. Fortunately for you, it is hard enough for he or she to control the information that they let out. It is nearly impossible to control the information that others know and release about them, so find a way in the circle and ask questions. Just don't overstep your boundaries.

Being Their Lover-When being a "player", there are certain rules that should not be broken. It works best if these rules are stuck to religiously and are not deviated from. These things are as follows:

1) Never give a title.- If you ever give a title you are no longer a player; you become a cheater. As long as you have no title you have no obligation. There were times where I had been found out by some of the women that I had been dealing with, but because I was not obligated to any one of them I was able to keep seeing all of them. Oh yeah, and they were all friends by the way.

2) Do not give out passwords to anything.- No security codes to

your house, no cell phone passwords, no email accounts, nothing. Limit all access they have. First of all, if you grant them access, at no point in time can you go back and restrict access without it bringing suspicion on yourself. It is a lot easier for him or her to say, "I've never had access to his stuff," versus "I used to have access but he changed all of his passwords." It brings unnecessary attention to the things you want to hide.

3) Establish roles and do not deviate from them.- If your relationship with your Lover is sexual, keep it sexual. If it is just to kick it at the jazz club on weekends, do just that. When you it switch up the dynamics of your relationship will change, which brings questions. As a player you will operate better with as few questions as possible, so when you start doing more with your partner the question of "What are we?" will come up. Doing less with your partner will bring up the question of, "What's going on with us?" Keep things as they are until you have decided to cut ties. Until then, do not change.

4) Control everything.- Timing, location, activities, EVERYTING. You need to be aware of who, what when, where,

why and how at all times. Any time you are not in control of these things, leaves the chance for something unexpected to happen. Unexpected could be good, but it can also be catastrophic.

5) Never engage someone who is smarter than you.- I'm not talking solely their level of aptitude. Being charming and charismatic works on most people, but when you see the person you are trying to court picking up tricks you are trying to pull, EJECT. Do not let pride be your downfall because as soon as one person knows your truth, there is no telling how many others will find out afterwards. It is okay to lose a battle as long as you are not losing the war.

Defense- Although there are a lot of rules to BEING a "player", there is but one rule that defends against their advances. Pay attention, be perceptive and do not write off the things you think are clear signs that you are getting played. When you start to notice something, keep an eye on it. Do not brush anything under the table. I have had plenty of women from my past tell me they would NEVER do something. My response is the same for them as it is for you: ANYTHING THAT SOMEONE HAS THE ABILITY TO DO, YOU MUST ACCEPT THAT THEY HAVE THE POSSIBILITY TO DO IT. That is to say that if a man or woman is capable (as in it does not defy some law of physics) then it is also possible that it can occur. Murphy's Law if you will. Do not be naive. Pay attention and watch to see what is going on in your relationship.

Cutting Ties-You must know when to cut ties. This may mean one person in particular, or this may mean everyone on your "roster." If you see something starting to topple, do not get caught in the debris. Reasons to cut ties: (1) someone who is about drama and putting things out in the public eye (via Facebook or other means) because they begins to suspect they are being played; or (2) someone who you are dating knows someone else you are close to. Things like this have the potential to out you as a "player" and can potentially ruin any further hopes you have at playing "the game." Your best option is to just cut ties and be done with the person altogether. If you are being figured out by more than one person, abandon ship. It is better to start over from scratch than it is to try and hold on to a sinking ship because you will go down with it.

Defense-There is no defense for someone who is a "player" and is cutting ties with you. If you have gotten to this point, unfortunately it means that you have already been a part of their "game." Cutting ties is the best course of action for you. The only option you have is to be the one who does it first. Trust me, its is for the best.

15

<u>The Love Drug</u>

I like to speak about love in terms that are easily relatable to subjects that people understand. Love has often been referred to as a drug and when you look at how it effects us, the comparison is not that crazy. The human body is constantly releasing chemicals into our brains in response to various stimuli. We are our own supplier. In search of a balance, these natural drugs create different effects in our system, physical and psychological manifestations that can occur in response to our interactions with our environment and each other. Love ensnares you, it owns you, it consumes you, it can make you do things you said you would never do. Love can be the thing that heals us or destroys us, depending on how we take it in. But let's take a second to talk about the Love drug, as it is, in its purest form.

The Act- Love is not a spectator sport and it REQUIRES participation. We engage in things that are considered "Acts of Love." These are the things that we feel constitute a cause to connect with someone else. If Love is a drug then the "Acts of Love" would be comparable to when you physically smoke or ingest the drug. Most often people associate these actions with being the actual drug. They are not. It is the means to the end or the mode to getting the high. The high comes from the emotion experienced from the act. How potent the emotion depends on the individual experiencing the drug and the act itself. While holding hands for one person may mean nothing, it can ignite a world of emotions for someone else. Sex has a vast range of emotional effects for various people. The actions are how you receive the emotion. For example, kissing someone does not mean that you love them, but kissing can lead to the expression of feelings that can lead to love. Just as there are a lot of ways to get high, there are numerous ways to connect with someone to get your Love high. Love is the top of the mountain, and there is more than one way to reach the top.

The High- Love can take you on high's you have never felt before. This is actually the part that we yearn for. This is the whole purpose for why we search for love. NOBODY SMOKES FOR THE SAKE OF SMOKING, THEY SMOKE FOR THE HIGH. In the same sense, "Acts of Love" are done for the emotional high given off as a consequence of someone's action. Everyone experiences different emotions when they are in Love, but the desire for it comes from the same source. After "Acts of Love" are committed Love energy begins to flow into us. Our willingness to accept that energy determines our perception of the high. Not everyone wants the high all the time. It hits us in phases, and everyone's phase doesn't not occur at the same time. But when experienced, Love brings on a euphoria that makes the world go away. The high hooks us and pulls us in.

The Side Effects-When in love the brain releases certain neurotransmitters, such as dopamine and norepinephrine, which affect the pleasure centers of the brain leading to positive "vibes" and feelings of excitement. Similar effects can come from the usage of amphetamines. The side effects ,the good, the bad, and the ugly. Depending on how we experience Love's high will determine what type of side effects we have.

The side effects are often determined IF the object or person we love returns those emotions to us. Spurned love can turn into resentment, bitterness, and so many other emotional problems that we may or may not be equipped to handle. When dealing with someone who we are unsure of how they feel, it is wise to guard or check our own emotions. Being aware of your Lover's perception of you helps to ease any negative effects that can come from your relationship.

It's not all dark clouds all the time. I have experienced the worst and the best of Love's side effects. Positive effects of the Love drug can act as a synergetic force. Both sides in a relationship can benefit from the energy passed between the two. The greatest part of loving someone is to be able to do so fully without fear of consequences. This is the purest high; the one that keeps you going for days that you never want to come down from. If you are going to have side effects, you want them to be positive ones.

Addiction- With all drugs there is the potential for addiction. The feelings are so powerful it is hard for us to become unattached to them. We struggle to separate ourselves from that feeling that we got a taste of. The sampling of something sweeter than our own bitter company. Some people get so fixated on finding love that nothing else matters. Some are groomed from a young age to find a good husband or get a wife and settle down, so łLove becomes an obsession and a very destructive one at that. You end up skipping over the steps necessary to formulate a healthy understanding of what you are getting into. This is like making heroin the first drug you ever try. If you go hard coming out the gate, then coming back to a state of normalcy will seem impossible. A lot of people continue to use drugs in search of that initial high that they experienced. If you cannot sustain the love that you have, everything else will seem secondary until you can find your internal balance and have a healthy understanding of how Love works.

Rehab- Through it all there is always a road to recovery. When you can't overcome love's hold on you, the first thing you need to do is be able to remove yourself. Step away from love and sober up for a bit. You can never see clearly when you are still engaged in the activity that has got you hooked. Tending to your emotional state must become routine and habitual. Everyone needs to do some emotional maintenance and reassessment every once in a while. If you make taking care of you a priority, then the next time you encounter instances of emotional lows you are less likely to drop. Surround yourself with people who also care about your emotional state. When recovering from Love's low points it is not good to be alone, but it is also not good to be around people who have nothing to support you and help you back up.

The last part of rehab is knowing that nothing is permanent. That even when things seem their worst, you can always try again. Soul mates are not one time occurrences, you can have many over one lifetime. Every experience you have in love is just that an experience, not a state of perpetual continuity. Don't be afraid to move forward. Love's high can be amazing. Take it for what it is and don't dwell on the negatives.

Ex Factor- *It's hard to get it out of our system sometimes. The feeling of love hooks us like fish on a line. We get a taste of something that we like and don't want to let it go. That's is how she was, so I will call her "The Fix."*

In all honesty I was her fix. She was going through an emotional time and I recognized that she was in a vulnerable state. She still wanted that same feeling, trying to get back to on that high. I knew sex was a sweet substitute for the real thing and I could easily take her mind off the hurt that she was going through. I just had to put myself in position.

I was mature for my age, so I was usually able to convince older women to give me a chance. She wasn't that much older but it usually doesn't take much for a woman to call you "a baby" compared to her. That same arrogance set her up for failure as she invited me over to spend time with her, which only resulted in us being intimate with each other. It was exactly what she needed, and just like that she kept coming back for more. She would call

all times of night and try to see me whenever her schedule

permitted. Any opening she could find to get her "fix" she would

take it. I was more than happy to be her supplier.

That was until I could tell things were getting more

serious than I wanted. As I saw her start to become more and

more attached, I knew it was time to make the last call on our

relationship. I cut her off, knowing that in the end she would be

better off. Sometimes you just need something to get you through

to the next.

16

It's All in Your Mind

Chance favors the prepared mind, and love itself at times is nothing more than a game of chance. In order to even the odds and tip the scales in your favor, you must be prepared for anything and everything.

The first stage of seduction is the seduction of the mind. I have found that in cases of romance, seduction or playing *the game*, that things tend to follow the same structure as Darwinism. The strongest and most aggressive dominate, and the weaker are left with the scraps. At the end of the night those who could not "seal the deal" with someone end up spending the night playing Xbox and watching Netflix until their weakness grants them the release of sleep.

"The strong" is a funny term when you think of it in regards to humans. Look at the literal application to mankind. We are not the strongest or the fiercest living creatures on this planet. Put any man in a cage with a fully grown lion or any number of wild animals, and I can tell you, the match will not end in a tie. However, humans are smart. We innovate, we invent and we create new ways to solve old problems, which that is how we have established an order where we are the dominant creatures on this planet. Why don't we do this when it comes to relationships? Whether man or woman, the thing that grants you the most power is not what is between your legs or under your shirt, but what is in your head. A woman with good looks can't hold a candle to a woman with good looks and a brain. Learning this will separate you from the rest of the Neanderthals when it comes to dating. You are the only caveman with fire because you made a decision to operate outside of your "basic" nature. All seduction starts in the mind, so thinking needs to be home base. It's time to brainstorm.

The Set Up: Have your mark in mind. There is no seduction without a goal. Going out saying, "I'm leaving with someone tonight," is desperate and stupid. Seduction is about leaving the situation with your power intact. Not achieving a momentary physical connection that leaves you lost or empty If you do not know who you are going for then you need to do a preparatory assessment; no different than casing a bank. You want to take your time and learn as much as possible about any potential option you may have. Remember, what you know, what you learn, empowers you. Some of the things you should check for:

Are they alone?

Do they seem approachable?

Are they busy at the moment?

If they are not alone that does not mean they cannot be approached. However, this should change your approach. I can tell you that a woman with a group of her friends must be approached delicately. Not acknowledging her friends can be asking for embarrassment. Try instead, complimenting the group and then asking to speak to the person of your interest.

Approachability is based not only on the person, but the environment and circumstances you are in. A guy that seems to be angry or in a bad mood may not necessarily want some girl flaunting her stuff in his face, no matter how good she looks. Also, a hot chick standing near the speakers at a concert may not get the full gist of your affections when you try to converse with her. Take this into account.

Sometimes it is better to hold off. Lie in wait until the right moment presents itself. There are men and women who DO NOT want to be approached in certain settings (which is probably the primary reason for them leaving). In these instances, you need to think about relocation before approach. Also, recognize when it is necessary to retreat.

Nothing ruins your chances more than approaching someone when they are in the middle of something else. If she's eating, LEAVE HER ALONE. If it's the fourth quarter of the Super Bowl (recognized as a national men's holiday), DO NOT bat your eyes at him. It will most likely go unnoticed and your feelings will be hurt. Timing is everything. Think before you sink.

Your approach should be thought out before you engage. I can guarantee that any woman I have ever approached I already had the first three conversational pieces in mind: introduce yourself, ask for their name, compliment, express your intentions, discuss their choice in food, etc.

Planning should never be too elaborate, mental seduction should seem natural. Your planning should be more of a guideline or a game plan Sometimes in sports you have to deviate from the original play in order to score. Playing "the game" should be no different. Be fluid with your thinking and adapt to the situation in a way that doesn't take away your advantage. You sit down with a guy and start a conversation just as he's paying for the bill. You haven't got to the point in the conversation that you can ask for a his phone number or give yours without looking desperate. Instead of letting things end, ask if he would like to join you or if you can walk with him to his car. Be fluid. Be ready for the situation to take a sharp turn at any moment. When you expect it, your change will seem natural. Remember chance favors the prepared mind.

      Listening- Most people listen without hearing. They receive the sounds without deciphering the meaning. I will tell you that conversation is where most people will give you all the ammunition that you need to seduce them. You have been given a simple system for approach. Understanding this gives you two things. First, you have the knowledge you need to get what you want or where you want. Second, you know how to defend yourself from being manipulated by being careful about what information you divulge in conversation. Don't just hear the words, hear the meaning. For example, you see a nice looking woman sitting at the bar alone and you ask her, "Are you here with anyone?" Her response is, "I wish." Now most people would just say, *Good. She's alone. I can approach.* What she really said was that she wishes she wasn't alone. That "I wish" meant that she wants someone that she could be with, someone to give her a reason to NOT be sitting at bars by herself. Things like; tone, body language (which I will discuss later) and more all give an answer to a question regarding who it is you are pursuing. Don't just hear the words, hear the meaning. The meaning is where you will be able to further your game plan and build your strategy.

Ex factor- *I love it when a plan comes together. Especially one that results in me benefitting more than I had expected to. I was on a brief, hiatus from my girlfriend at the time due to some unresolved issues she had with faithfulness. During my break I decided I wouldn't just wait around for her to get it together. I would explore some options that were currently lying on the table. I was home from college for Christmas break and had on Facebook, I contacted a girl I will call "the Substitute."*

She stayed in the dorm across the street from mine, but we had never spoken in person. She was a little more plain than the average women I had dealt with. I was in a position of wanting to make my "girlfriend" mad at the time, so looks didn't particularly matter. As I continued to speak with "the Substitute" she gave me all the information I needed to get into her mind. She told me what her turn-ons were, she told me where to touch her to get her riled up...she pretty much handed me the keys to the city and begged me to take it.

We made plans to get together when we got back to school. She even said she would be willing to come back to school a day early so that we could hang out. So I did. When eChristmas break ended, I arrived on campus and within 15 minutes of being there I closed the deal. Like I said, I Love it when a plan comes together.

STRATEGY VS TACTICS

A lot of people confuse the two. Some people never implement them when it comes to Love and "the game," some just react. If you are quick witted and charming, that may work for you some of the time, but not all the time and not for everyone. Mental seduction is about establishing a strategy and being tactical about the achievement of certain goals. Doing this in relationships helps to establish a good foundation for you to come back to, whether things are good are bad. This is home base.

Strategies have an overall end goal Your goal can be as

simple as getting the girl in the VIP section to have sex with you, or it can be as drawn out as getting married within five years. Along with your end goal, you will have smaller intermittent goals. If your goal is a one night stand, then your intermittent goal would be to get her name, gain her interest, etc. If your end goal is marriage, then your intermittent goal may be to get a first date. Your end goal is going to be determined by YOUR individual want's and needs. Whatever your strategy is, make sure it is defined and unchanging. If your strategy changes, it should only be under extreme circumstances. Usually those circumstances are cause for aborting the whole operation. The reason your goal should remain unchanged is because it is the guideline for all of your other plans and the basis for your mental seduction. If your goal is to get married and you change that to a more casual dating scenario, it can confuse both you and the person you are dating. It also shifts all actions and plans that were aligned with that particular goal. Your actions initially were more in line with commitment and longevity, but now that you have decided to go with something less serious. Unless this is being done with the intention of confusing someone (which wouldn't be a change in strategy. It causes you to be more reactionary and you are no longer planning out how you're are going to do things. You are becoming an after effect of the circumstances that act upon your life. You have strayed from the beaten path into new territory that you are most likely not prepared for. Chaos ensues and you fail.

Tactics are how you operate when engaged or interacting with someone. If your goal is to get married, then you use tactics to get you there. They are the bullet points in your presentation. Tactics can change or they can be stagnant. They are situational and predetermined. Thinking tactically is thinking on your feet and knowing that even when things aren't going according to the plan, they are still going as planned.

End goal: One night stand. Tactically, in order to pull this off you have to get her to agree with this idea. This can be done by buying drinks, stimulating conversation, gaining trust or creating comfort (the ingredients necessary to achieve your goal). Encourage a rendezvous and have a place already in mind prior to suggesting the rendezvous. Offer to drive and have a place prepared. SCORE....

You always want to minimize the work being done in real time. PRE-WORK is important. It is what creates the smoothness, the natural feeling and what inspires awe and mesmerizes your target. The reason you want to do your pre-work is because things don't always work the way you want. If you plan to use music, have it already on a playlist so you can easily access it so all you have to do is hit play when the moment is right. Don't fumble trying to create one and search for songs or wait for iTunes to update. Every second wasted takes you further away from your goal. The further out your end goal is, the smaller your intermittent goals should be.

If sex is your end goal, there can't really be big intermittent goals. All you can do is say things like, "Hey wanna come to my place for a drink?" or, "Can I call you sometime?" There is plenty of tactical planning that can go into trying to reach sex as the end goal, but ultimately there are very few achievable goals between meeting them and having sex in the same night, unless you count things like the first time you and your date held hands, or your firs kiss, first time having oral sex and so on. For most adults if you get to oral sex, intercourse is guaranteed. I've made the mistake of waiting a long time just to get sex from someone (my pride wouldn't let me quit). When you wait too long you eventually run out of intermittent goals and end up repeating attempts at your end goal until you either give up or you reach it.

Marriage for an end goal can have big intermittent goals because it is generally a longer process. Just be sure not to show your trump card too early if the other person is unaware of your intentions, or they may be able to work against it. With long term goals, your intermittent goals should be similar things, such as go on a few dates, meet their friends, become exclusive, meet the family, discuss marriage, etc.

When you make planning for in a relationship (and a one night stand is a relationship with an extremely short duration) a priority you can seamlessly move and operate within it. Your lover will adore being with you because things seem easy, which makes it easy for them. Assess your target/situation, set a goal, form a strategy, set smaller goals, and achieve them tactically. Do these things and I guarantee you will find that relationships hold a new bearing in your mind. The more thought you put into how you're are going to approach it makes you have to think less when you are actually in it. I've said it many times, chance favors the prepared mind. It's time to get prepared.

17

<u>Seducing the Senses</u>

The second stage of seduction is the physical stage. Once again, remember the three parts of seduction and how they are all intertwined. The physical stage is the doorway into the emotional part of seduction. It is necessary to accomplish these, in order, so you can achieve the desired effect. I like to breakdown this process by using the five senses to illustrate the modes of seduction.

<u>Sight-</u>They say the eyes are the doorways to the mind and soul. This is very true when you think about how the eye can literally transmit millions of pieces of information to the brain in a matter of seconds. The brain also recognizes things that are seen as aesthetically pleasing to us. We know what we like when we see it. Even on a non-attraction level, we still know what we find to be appealing to our brain. For example, the brain naturally finds things that are symmetrical to be more appealing therefore, unconsciously you would pay less attention to things that are not symmetrical.

Visual seduction is probably the one that most everyone is familiar with. That's is why I chose to discuss this one first, as it is not a necessarily new concept. We all think to put on a sexy outfit, or work out, or wear those jeans that show off our butt a little bit more. Men and women can have similar and completely contrasting views on how to appeal to the visual aspects of someone's pleasure center. Visual attraction, for most people, is a psychological trigger based on what you are attracted to. Psychologically a man who is around or has usually interacts with larger women is more likely to be attracted to larger women. A woman who has always dated men of darker complexions will most likely find darker skinned men attractive. The brain is programmed easily by repetitious behavior. It's not hard to see how the things we are attracted to fit into our life, and how the visualization of these characteristics can affect us.

Overall, people recognize the traits the brain automatically registers as "attractive." These would be things such as nice eyes, beautiful lips, etc. But this is surface level attraction and seduction REQUIRES you go deeper. Not all men want a woman who looks like a runway model, not all women want a man who is built like a linebacker. To each their own. Understanding this is critical to the visual seduction process. You must know what the person LIKES to see. Just because you think something is cute does not mean it will get the attention of the one you are trying to seduce. Seduction requires you to think about someone else's wants in order to get what you want. In appealing to the visual aspects of someone's desires you must be realistic and know what will work for you. What is sexy for some is not sexy for all. However, anyone can bring their own sexy to the table.

Guy A: *Very simple, likes his woman to wear an oversized T-shirt and nothing else. Drives him wild.*

Woman A: *Wanting to be sexy for him, spends $40 on a lingerie* *set that she is sure will make him lose it.*

Scenario: Guy A doesn't much care for the lingerie but knows she was trying, so he goes along with her little show as to not hurt her feelings. They have sex but the desire created was not the same. It feels routine. Girl A feels disappointed because she did not get the reaction she wanted. Overall satisfaction level= Average

The issue here was that in trying to seduce, Woman A went with what *she* thought made her sexy versus what *he* thought made her sexy. Remember, seduction is about giving the other person what they want so you can get what you want. In relationships it is important for both parties to feel sexy because of self-esteem reasons. However, when you are attempting to seduce someone, you are putting your feelings aside to achieve a goal. You have an agenda and feelings of appreciation should not be a priority.

Girl B: *A hopeless romantic who has always wanted to make Love on a bed covered in rose petals.*

Guy B:*Wants to surprise his fiancé with a romantic evening as well as get her in a good mood so he can ask her about going to a friend's bachelor party that weekend. He knows how much she has always wanted a bed full of rose petals to make Love on. He sets the scene*

Scenario: Fiancé comes home to find a trail of rose petals leading to the bedroom. As she slowly follows the trail her excitement (and desire) continues to build. Her lover is sitting beside the bed, the scene set. She wants him more than she has ever wanted him before.

Guy B understood that by seducing his fiancé, he would be more likely to get what it was that he wanted. But in order to get his, he had to put her desires first. We are naturally inclined to do something for someone who has done something for us. When our lover acts in this manner, we give in to their desires because they have satisfied ours. Well played.

Taste- Taste is a fun one. When using taste as a method of seduction it can happen literally at any point you encounter the person. Food creates a pleasurable sensation in the brain and seduction is all about pleasure. We have all heard the old saying, "the fastest way to a man's heart is through his stomach."

Well it may not get you to his heart, but it sure makes the path a

lot easier. A lot of people want to take the aphrodisiac route, and

that may work for some people. However, what I'm going

to speak on is how simple foods (well prepared) can work

towards creating pleasure in the mind of the person you are trying

to seduce.

You can go two routes: A special meal or sensual foods. A

special meal is simply just a meal that would be highly

appreciated by the person you are trying to seduce. For example,

you know they love seafood, so you take them to the best seafood

restaurant in town, or even better, you prepare their favorite

seafood meal. Restaurants stand the chance of ruining the

ambiance with bad service, so they do not share your same goals

of seduction, they may not put the same level of importance on

meal preparation. When the meal is consumed, it tugs at the

emotions because the meal is important and you made it a

priority. If you can control the flow of emotions you have already

won half the battle.

The second route is sensual foods. This can be done during intercourse or it can be done in a sensual environment. Pick foods that are easily handled and require little preparation. Strawberries, chocolate and honey are some of my favorites. These foods should be chosen by 1)flavor, 2) texture, and 3) effect. Whether you and your Lover are sitting on the couch, feeding each other or stripped bare satisfying each other's palate, the food must have aspects that are appealing to the person you want to seduce. Look into their tastes beforehand as you do not want to go into planning a romantic evening only to find out your lover is allergic to citrus fruits. It is hard to seduce someone when you put them in the emergency room.

Everyone has different tastes, things that appeal to their palate. Learn these important details, and study them. Sweet foods, spicy foods, whatever they like, have it ready in abundance. Texture matters because you also want whatever goes into their mouths to FEEL pleasurable. Avoid rough and grainy foods. It should be sexy, smooth and sensual to the touch as well as the taste. This is seduction, there are places where it is okay to be rough around the edges, But feeding your ~~l~~Lover isn't one of them.

Lastly, you should select your foods for effect. Do you want to tease her slowly, allowing her to feed as she wants to? Do you intend to feed him allowing him to taste the food, as well as you-? Some foods seem sexy but end up being messy. Plan out how you want the evening to go then serve up the Loving that your partner wants.

Sound- The sweetest sound heard by in any language is a person's name. One of the easiest methods of auditory seduction is the intentional whispers of your name by your lover. There is a difference between "I love you" and "I love you, Amy." It personalizes, it adds feeling, it makes everything real. Make it deliberate, make it passionate. Say the name of the person you want to want you.

There are also supplementary sounds that are pleasurable to the ear. Listening to music during intimate moments increases the release of feel-good hormones in the brain. The music itself should be well thought out, low in volume, smooth in transition and non-distracting (like elevator music, except this won't drive you crazy). I myself was a musician and I can liken the creation of the perfect song to making love…the rhythm, the mood, the emotion. It is all laid out so you can seduce your audience.

In your case, seducing your audience of one should be much easier. One of the greatest sounds ever is the natural sounds of making love to the person you want to be with. Just be careful about what sounds you allow. Control any "unattractive sounds", like that weird laugh you make during sex that could potentially ruin the moment. Control what goes into their minds.

Smell- The most subtle and possibly the most important of all the senses to control. On a very basic level we emit pheromones that indicate our desire to be intimate with someone. This is uncontrollable for the most part, as these are secreted through our bodily fluids (which we tend to wash off). On a more controllable level, certain aromas appeal to the olfactory systems of the brain. Pleasure is the purpose. So when you smell something that smells good or that your partner thinks smells good, pleasure is received. DON'T drown yourself in cologne or bathe in perfume. Find a scent that they like spray it *lightly* in the area they will be as well as on your body. Smell is important. Seduction is like hunting and most animals hunt using their sense of smell. Do not underestimate the power of an erotic aroma.

Touch- Touch is powerful. It is the EASIEST method of seduction because we are naturally inclined to touch the person that we want. Seductive touch should start long before intimacy begins. That means gently grabbing butts, sneaking kisses, skin to skin contact. This is the set up.

With intimacy, touch is important as long as it is the RIGHT touch. You need to know: WHEN, WHERE, AND HOW to touch your lover if you want to successfully seduce them using physical contact. "When" means being in touch with them enough to understand timing. If your woman is slowly unwinding by a kiss, do not automatically go straight for her lower regions. Everything must be done with time.

"Where" on the body is extremely important. Everyone has "spots" or erogenous zones that incite erotic feelings and build attraction. Every person's zones are different. Because one woman likes to be kissed on the ear does not mean EVERY woman does. Not all men have the same levels of comfort with certain types of physical contact. It is important to understand the needs and wants of your lover. Ask, "Where is your favorite place to be kissed?", "What places are off limits?", and "Can I have free reign to touch where I want?" These things are important to you because they determine the "comfort" level of your lover. Trust isn't necessary, but comfort is if you want to be able to successfully seduce ANYONE.

"How" is the next part and also just as important as where. Knowing where someone likes to be touched is just a portion of the battle. "How" is also determined by the individual. It is not a generic. It cannot be categorized. DO NOT SKIP OUT ON VITAL INFORMATION THAT IS NECESSARY FOR SEDUCTION. How someone wants to be touched plays heavily into their psychology. The way someone wants to be touched is reflective of how they want to be loved. Gentle or rough, we all like to be touched.

Ex Factor- I will call her "the *Bronx."- She was around* *five feet, two inches tall, of Latin seduction and I was infatuated with the newness that she introduced into my life. Drowning in the smell of perfume and pheromones, my senses failed to register anything beyond her beauty. She was aggressive, which was something I wasn't used to. I was new to this whole game of love and she was a veteran. She would whisper in my ear in her native tongue, all while caressing my body. She attacked all of my senses at the same time (a trick that I would later learn to use for myself).*

I wanted her and she knew it. She exploited the fact that she could pull me in with just a word. I was putty in her hands. I was the newborn barely walking while she could run a sexual marathon with me and reminded me constantly of that fact. I broke the rules, for her sake. She brought a sense of excitement that transformed my thinking. Public displays of affection, deep kisses in the elevator, skipping out to mess around. I was absorbed into her sexual essence. The funny thing is we never had sex. I was her puppet, and I loved every moment. She created an environment in which the only thing I was able to perceive was her. Like hypnosis, I was under her spell. When she was around there was nothing but her. Her scent filled my nose, her voice rang in my ears, I couldn't take my eyes off her, and her touch held me captive. It is funny, in controlling my senses, she essentially left me...senseless.

The senses are the doorways to our emotions being triggered. We tie our feelings to certain things that we perceive from our environment. Remember, most people operate in the pursuit of pleasure, so our willingness to accept the things that bring us pleasure is typically higher with someone we are comfortable with. That willingness is what you are banking on and is vital to the success of your seduction. So ignite their senses and set your love aflame.

18

<u>Leaving a legacy</u>

The mind is an interesting thing. It plays an amazing part in romantic relationships. Once you comprehend it, you can understand yourself. Think of a time when you were hurt, where you fell, or broke a leg, or scraped yourself and you remember that it hurt. You may remember crying, but the physical pain associated with it fades. Think also of a time where you ate a food you liked, or a first kiss, or even your first sexual experience. The memories are the same. You don't remember the physical pleasure, just the emotions tied with it. The feelings stay with us.

Emotional seduction is the most volatile of the three seduction types. As with any form of seduction, you must have a goal in mind. The goal should be to be remembered. To be immortalized forever in the hearts of those who experienced your love. Whether it is a one night stand or a five year affair, they must remember. However,they won't remember you for how great your sex was. People always assume that what keep people coming after them is the physical aspects. Men and women both commit physical acts for the emotions that come from them. The emotion may be the pride of conquering a woman who was believed to be untouchable, it may be the calming power of a woman's caress, it can be the closeness that is felt. Remember, think of Love as a drug. If sex is the act of smoking, the emotions experienced would be "the high." Nobody smokes for the sake of smoking, they do it for the feeling. The same goes for physical Love. It's the high that keeps us. We are all in search of the most potent drug to keep us hooked.

So how do you tie the emotions of one being to the love of another? It's not as simple as uttering a magic word (I love you doesn't always cut it). You have to do two things: you must be able to disarm and you must be able to control emotional flow between you and your Love.

Disarming someone can happen honestly or using the methods previously discussed. Everyone has an emotional dam that holds back emotions from flowing freely and spilling into our day to day lives. If someone were to be nothing more than a big mass of feelings, they would hardly be able to function. Emotions flow out from us. We choose who to release them to as if slowly raising our own flood gates. Emotional seduction means you hold the key to someone else's flood gates.

There are a few methods you can use to control the emotional flow between you and someone else. The first is selfless action: doing things for someone with no PERCEIVED benefit. These things should be done without being prompted by any person, event, or request. This is to give the appearance of genuineness. It can actually be genuine depending on your reasons. Not all seduction has ill intent. You can seduce those you love as well. Seduction is simply the means to a very sensual end.

Some people seek only to grow closer emotionally with

their lover. Emotional seduction is about the control of emotional flow between two people, so it goes without saying that your emotions can also be involved. When you commit these selfless actions they should be things that also matter to the other person. So ladies, making dinner when you *always* make dinner doesn't register as a special event nor as a selfless action to your man. It seems as though you are looking for praise by doing something for him. No matter how much you say, "I did this for you", the truth is you did it for self.

There are people, both men and women, who do things solely so they can make themselves look great or someone else look bad. Be wary of these people. If you are doing something for someone else it should be FOR them. Guys, do not buy her tickets to *your* favorite rock band's concert, that would make you the world's biggest jerk. Ladies, don't buy him an outfit that *you* thought was cute. He's your man, not a Ken doll.

Put them first and do the act without expectation of reward or perceived benefit. If there is a reward to be had from your actions, do not let it become known. Buy her a spa day for no reason. Get him basketball tickets to see his favorite team. In doing this, you have created an emotional need for them to reciprocate the action and do something for you. But by you putting things in motion, you have begun to tug at that emotional rope. Your stock just rose in their eyes.

Ex Factor- *When someone wears their heart on their sleeve, it's pretty much low hanging fruit. Emotions make us vulnerable to both pain and manipulation. I can definitely say that for some women, it becomes more important to put it all out there; because of their age. As they see their lives continue on without hitting the milestones, like getting married and having kids, they feel the pressure of growing old alone and that fear expedites their actions. But in rushing, you take away your ability to think clearly. For a guy like me, that's what I want, is for you to want something so bad you would forgo logic to ensure it happens.*

I will call her "Juliet," because she was always searching for her Romeo. In her mid-thirties, she had indicated to me how important it was for her to find a husband SOON. She was a caramel creature and was very easy on the eyes. She was looking for her prince charming, so I just had to pretend that was who I was and I would earn my way into her heart.

On the first date we kissed, creating a wave of emotion and yearning in her that showed in her eyes. Like a child wanting a toy she saw in the store window, her desire for me was sealed. She then proceeded to ask, "What are we?" I answered her without answering "I really like you, I'd like to keep seeing you, etc." Empty promises of caring for her spat out for the sake of keeping her locked on me.

She was cool but was too easily manipulated. If I could play with your emotions this easily, then I knew a woman couldn't pose a mental challenge for me in a relationship. I knew that I just had to string her along long enough to get what I wanted. However she held that "asset" from me for quite some time, longer than I wanted to actually be bothered with it. So, in order to get what I wanted, I tugged at her heart strings. I told her, "I could see us being in a relationship," and that I really cared for her. I made her believe she was the only one. I made these *promises while activating her emotions through physical action. Intimacy tied with conversation usually leads to words forgotten or misinterpreted. Reason overlooked, she gave in. With my goal accomplished, I made up an excuse to stop seeing her. Leaving her, and her emotions, in tatters.*

An excellent way to be the "happy drug" is to continually strive to make your partner happy. Make every moment possible, a happy moment. This means not arguing, listening to their problems, doing the sweet gushy stuff that everyone complains about yet still keeps doing. Basically become their personal Make-a-Wish Foundation. You should be their yes man (or woman) as often as possible, but still try to maintain control of the scenario.

Exceed expectation- The expectations in question of course would be those of the person you are trying to seduce. This is easiest when the person you are seducing has already low expectations of you or the relationship. These are the people who have preset notions of what occurs in relationships either from what they have been told in the past or what they have experienced. However, these situations must also be handled delicately because people who have low expectations of romantic success tend to want to give up easily. Most people express their concerns in a relationship early on., but if they do not tell you, ask. This knowledge is key to your success.

The drawback- Emotional seduction, as I previously stated, is risky. In essence, you are playing with fire anytime you place bets on someone else's feelings. Not everyone has a need for emotional seduction. Assess the type of person you are dealing with first. If you know that this someone is in an extremely delicate emotional state you can assume you would. Also, be aware of your emotional state as well. As you grow closer to your target there becomes a mixing of emotions between the two of you. You can completely cut off emotional connection with them and focus on your romantic goals. However, there is a higher chance of you being "found out" and you will fail to properly adjust the flow of emotions between the two of you.

Emotional flow should be seen as a kinetic energy source. It builds and it grows as it is shifted between yourself and your partner. Energy is not destroyed or lost according to the law of the conservation of energy, it just changes form. In the same sense, when you do not continue the flow of energy between yourself and your partner, that energy becomes an action. An action that is probably contrary to your goals of seduction. So keep the emotions flowing, but in a controlled manner and in a direction that favors your desires.

19

<u>True Lies</u>

<u>Disclaimer</u>: Deceit used in relationships has the potential to destroy any form of trust held. It ultimately can end not just romantic dealings with someone, but can ruin any relationship you could potentially have in the future. Use at your own discretion.

<u>Ex Factor-</u> *Deception is an art. The whole purpose is to gain an advantage. To reap the spoils. Sometimes there are innocent bystanders who get caught up in the game. I will call her "The Virgin," as that was what she was when we met.*

A small girl from the Philippines with a sweet smile and a pure heart. Usually I avoided those types. I was not one for being the cause of a good girl gone bad. But from our first conversation, I could tell she was interested in me, and my ego wouldn't let her slip away. Her friend, who was around when we met, knew who I was. I could tell as I introduced myself that she recognized my name. Fortunately, "The Virgin" didn't know me, so I intended to keep her distracted by charming conversation. I got her number and invited her over to watch movies.

During the first movie we kissed. I believe it was actually her first kiss. She liked the feel and wanted more. I could've flexed my reputation; on someone with a little experience, but in order to not scare her off I downplayed it. I had to take it slow because her uncertainty as to how she wanted to proceed made the situation very precarious.

After hours of tiptoeing around the idea, we agreed to try to be intimate, but I had never been anyone's first time. I could not finesse the situation as I had in prior encounters. Out of frustration of not being able to control the pace, we decided to not go to that level. I had gotten the most that I could out of that situation. A lot more than I would've gotten had I not controlled *the information she had about me. Your reputation can make you or break you. In this instance it was better if she didn't know who she was getting in bed with.*

Love and war. To think of these items as separate entities is a mistake. They are different sides of the same coin. In war you are either fighting to gain ground or to protect what ground you have. Love is the same. We attempt to advance our romantic agendas or we hide behind the walls of our heart and hope to protect the sanctity of our emotions. Strategy and tactics. Planning and more planning. Battles of the heart hard fought for the purpose of fulfilling some desire, some need. Passion can only get you so far. Learning how to win without ever having to fight is the prime example of evolving your game. Deception is the key to winning a war.

The greatest victories in war are from the battles that someone doesn't even know they are fighting. In relationships, the person you are with is not an opponent but they are an opposing force. You want something from them. They are the only thing stopping you from getting what you want, so your goal is to remove the opposition. In playing "the game" you NEVER rely on the generosity of the person you are pursuing. They owe you nothing and this method of thinking will usually leave you with nothing. What I'm teaching you is how to earn each meal every moment is what you deserve which gives you more control and is far more rewarding.

Distract-Misdirection is my favorite form of deception. It is the magic of romantic manipulation. Show them one thing but give them something else. While their focus is on other matters, you are slowly achieving your goals. When you witness a magic trick it's all sleight of hand. Smoke in mirrors and pyrotechnics; the key is keeping the focus on something other than you.

Sex is one of the easiest distractions to enact on someone and it is also one of the riskiest. Everything fades away during intercourse. However, sometimes the thing you want to do is distract someone from the fact that sex is what you are after. Or maybe you want to distract someone without having to rely on sex because sex is always a gamble. You can distract someone by doing a few different things:

1) *Appealing to their emotions*- If you can actively cause an emotional response from someone, you can distract them from your true intentions. Emotions can cloud judgement; however, emotions come with consequences of their own. In past relationships I would often start empty arguments for the sake of getting a woman so riled up she can't think about anything other than the argument. All the while I moved forward with my own agenda. Emotions are interesting things, as we discussed before, they can cripple us or they can empower us. How you choose to use them is up to you.

2) *The unknown*-Not as often used, but still just as effective. Everyone has pre-judgements that they make, about people, places and events. We can't help it. Our concern for the unknown allows for the mind to wander. Sometimes it is to a good place, other times not so good. When we don't know something it can eat away at us because with unknowns there are possibilities and consequences we may not like.

Using the unknown also has to play to the personality of the one you wish to deceive. Do not divulge certain information upon interaction with someone. Never express your interest. They will be so consumed with the *what-if's* that they will forgo logic allowing you to do whatever you desire. Women use this a lot. Men approach women with the hopes of bedding them, women know what the man wants but has an alternative mission. Maybe she wants concert tickets, or entry into a club, maybe she wants a bill paid or maybe she wants a relationship. No matter what it is, if she can dangle that *what-if* in front of her suitor long enough he will be so focused on the possibility that he won't even see what's happening in reality.

3) *Appealing to their interest*-Know what your target wants and give it to them (or pretend to), so you can get what you want. People are more amicable when they are given what they want. They are more likely to do for you and less likely to resist you when they think you are satisfying their desires. But in this sense if you give an inch, they take a mile.

You must be willing to *sacrifice* something but doesn't mean you always will. However, the person in question must believe you will. For example, the promise of marriage you keep pledging knowing you are only staying because of convenience. - It happens a lot. You have to bait them enough to keep 'em biting, then when you have what you want reel 'em in.

Disarm-Lowering someone's guard can be challenging at times. Everyone believes it is about establishing trust. It's about comfort control. A person can trust you but be uncomfortable, and a person cannot trust you but still feel comfortable. Trust is established over time. Sometimes you don't have that, so instead you decide to work around their level of comfort. Blow the horn that will bring down the walls of Jericho.

Comfort is the defining point in all actions we do in relationships. We love when we feel comfortable, have sex, introduce to family and friends, essentially every major moment in ANY relationship is defined by our comfort level. So in order to disarm someone you must build an aura of comfort. They may not trust you. There were plenty of women who knew my reputation and still allowed me in because I made them feel comfortable. The same can happen for you. Like a wolf in sheep's clothing, you become close to the flock and you gain access to the most intimate parts of their lives.

Downplay-The challenge here is not drawing attention to yourself. With distractions, you must substitute your attention for something else. To disarm you must create a presence of comfort. But when you downplay you make moves that no one knows you are making. Let me say it again, that to do this you must make sure NOBODY knows the moves you are making.

A lot of people are bad liars. Only lie in circumstances where you have to explain or justify your actions. You should never be in a situation where you have to do this. It either means you are answering to someone or you got caught. If your goal is to deceive, your actions must be completely hidden. The best way to do this is to not bring it up. Don't mention you are going out, just go. This is the out-of-sight, out-of-mind form of deception. How can someone question something another does and do not suspect something going on? Move independently and do not involve others and you will be able to achieve a lot more.

Lying itself is an art form which is why not everyone is good at it Learning to lie with the truth is to be masterful. It is the ultimate form of deception.

Lying with the truth actually involves every one of the three aforementioned techniques. The truth itself usually helps to disarm. Given enough truth and disarming someone will not even be necessary. The truth given will distract from the intended goal. Downplaying your actual intentions happens much easier when given a false truth.

I had been with more women by age 25 than some men see in a lifetime. This is a fact, my truth. A truth that I often used to create the web that I used to deceive so many. Not every woman that I was seeing were tricked by deceptive practices, many of which were attempts at love gone bad.

As the numbers rose I realized something: some truths, no matter how "bad," appeal to us. Like a train wreck, you just have to watch. When I approached a woman and charmingly told her, "I couldn't be serious because of my past and who I was ," they smiled, nodded as if they understood. I think that was hope in throe eyes. But the truth was in their face; they distracted them from my purpose. I wanted something and I knew my truth was just enough to keep their interest while I procured it. Some would ask questions, some would say maybe you haven't found the right one. I knew that at that point in my life it didn't matter who it was, I would not settle. The right one didn't matter because I was the wrong one. This is what I told them, and they came flocking regardless.

Offering the truth is like an olive branch asking the other person to trust you. It shows vulnerability which opens most people up. People are more likely to share with you when you share first. Select the truth that would be appetizing to them, and let them feast on it while you eye the main course.

The truth is something mankind has always sought. The truth of ourselves, of who we are. The questions that need answering. The when's and the where's and the why's and the what's. A truth can be valuable. Hold on to your truths. Be careful what truth you share because the truth is a double edged sword. It can wound or heal. Do not be caught in its swing.

20

<u>Unfaithful</u>

First let's define cheating. This is not when the guy you like goes out with another girl. It is not when the girl you gave your number to gives her number to someone else. It is NOT when you have sex with someone only to find they are dating other people. It is when a relationship consisting of two people who have decided to be exclusive, and one of the two becomes involved with an outside party. Notice that I did not say have sex with, or kiss, or spend the night with.

Most people feel cheating is the worst thing that can happen in any relationship. Trust is betrayed, hearts are broken, love is lost. But in all these situations there is more than one responsible party. In fact there are always three parties involved in any case of infidelity. The person being cheated on(primary lover), the person that is cheating(the initiator), and the person they cheated with, or as I like to call them, the catalyst.

Cheating arises due to a need, one that varies between males and females. In 95% of situations they occur over time. Most people when they do cheat do so because there is something that they feel they can get from that other person. Sometimes these people are right. Not right in the sense that cheating is okay but right because they recognized a deficiency in their relationship and wanted to fill a void. The issue is they filled the void with someone other than their lover.

There are also times a person cheating feels they are missing something that really isn't. I have encountered countless people who cheated because they felt their relationship needed something but rather than communicating with their lover about this need they end up going elsewhere. How do you know your lover isn't willing to incorporate new things in their relationship unless you ask?

A lion, when full, does not needlessly hunt prey. It doesn't stalk the gazelle unless it is prompted to satiate a need. Basic. Humans are no different. The issue comes for us when we try to determine which need is going unattended. A man, when fully satisfied sexually, may still look at a woman because it is in our nature to desire them. Thanks testosterone. However, desire does not always prompt action. Every attractive woman doesn't provoke a sexual response. You must recognize when something is an actual threat or a perceived threat. A lot of women see all other women as threats. Sometimes the biggest threat to your relationship is yourself. Men are just as bad becoming overly possessive of a person they cannot possess. When you try to restrict what your woman can do, she becomes Rapunzel, locked away in a castle waiting for the first prince she can find to liberate her. You have created the motive for her to cheat on you.

Primary lover- This is is the person getting cheated on. The reason they are primary is because the catalyst, or person who cheats with the initiator, becomes secondary. The role they play in this scenario is vital because they create a circumstances where cheating is made possible. Is this to say they made them do it? That it is a fault of the primary lover? No. But if a child were to eat cookies left out by the parent, it could only happen if the parents make it accessible.

The goal for anyone in a relationship should be complete saturation. This means that when any need is asked about, the only logical answer is you. Who do you enjoy talking to? Who would you like to share your intimate moments with? Who do you think of late at night? The reality is that most couples do not think of their significant other for the answer to all of these questions. However, the closer you are to that point, the better your relationship will be. Think of a relationship as a band. You are the guitar player and your lover is the drummer. When you get close to complete saturation you are making beautiful music together. Reading each other's cues, everyone's on beat, making something wonderful. But when you aren't, your guitar playing clashes with the drums. You play fast, they play slow. You play softly and they bang hard. What you have created is something that doesn't sound good. Ultimately,bands that play this way end up replacing band members. Get on the same frequency, feel each other out, because if you don't, I can guarantee one of you will begin the search for someone who can match their frequency.

The cheater, or initiator, has either one of two problems: lack of focus or lack of relationship restraint, all those who cheat have one of these as the cause for their infidelity. If you are easily distracted from your relationship you lack relationship focus. Now we all what a P.O.A. is, is not an excuse for your infidelity. If you are wise, you found someone with traits that attracts you. If your partner does not possess those traits you may have "settled" and can be prone to cheating. Those who lack focus in their relationships are very simple to read. They are the ones who can only stay focused on the person they are with when that person is around. Like relationship attention deficit disorder, initiators can see someone else who is appealing and be pulled in. They are often the ones who say it is not their fault that they cheated and blames someone else.

Those with a lack of restraint, occurs when people are put in situations that could lead to cheating and they do not resist. I myself have been put in some hard positions, and still managed to resist. People with low restraint thresholds usually don't control their relationships and succumb to the wiles of more dominant forces. Stand your ground, temptation does not stop coming at you. You will be tempted by those who pursue you and won't have to do the work. These are the people who justify their cheating by saying, "It just happened." You need to strengthen your ability to resist.

The last part of the puzzle is the catalyst. I won't spend much time on them because there is a whole chapter dedicated to this role. But for now, the catalyst or the person who is cheating with the initiator, is the whole reason for this chapter. Without them cheating does not exist. The catalyst does not represent just the person, it represents all opportunities afforded that allow for cheating. However, not all catalyst are knowing or willing. Some actually go along believing they are the primary lover. Be mindful of your role and how someone views you in a relationship.

The formula for infidelity

Low risk + high reward (motivation) + catalyst (opportunity) ÷

time

First, understand that this is an expression. It becomes an equation or it actually equals something when you can plug in values for all the places.

If R = risk

M = motivation

C = catalyst

T = time

You can say R+M+C/T is the formula for infidelity.

 <u>**Risk-**</u> This should actually be the perceived risk. Anytime you cheat there is an actual risk. However, the perceived risk is what plays into someone making the decision to cheat. The biggest risk that is considered by both men and women is...WILL I GET CAUGHT? Other risks are things such as financial obligations, potential for feelings to grow, catching an STD and more. But the perception of the risk is what is factored into the decision.

Example 1: Johnny is planning to mess with the new intern at work, Veronica. Veronica had a wild past in college

while pledging to her sorority and has a long list of sexual partners. But she doesn't share that with Johnny. He doesn't see a risk because as far as he knows, she's just the hot new girl. They go into an empty cubicle and get it on.

Example 2: Johnny has always had a thing for his girlfriend's cousin, Stephanie At a pool party Johnny hosts, Stephanie walks up behind Johnny and puts her hands down his trunks. Johnny's girlfriend is in the other room. As perfect as this situation is, the risk is too high. He refuses and they go their separate ways.

Motivation- Motivation can be internal or external in regards to cheating. If the motivation is internal it is always negative and if it is external it is always positive. Internal motivators are always the negative aspects of your relationship. These are things like lack of respect, withholding sex, too many arguments or being boring. Anything that pushes your lover away can literally be the cause of cheating. The determining factor is the individual experiencing them. For instance, while one woman may be completely satisfied by being at home watching Netflix with her boyfriend another may be completely turned off by his unimaginative take on love. She would most likely seek out someone to give her the excitement her lover doesn't provide.

External motivation is always a positive trait. If the motivation is external it must mean that it is strong enough (or appealing enough) to make someone forget their current situation. The woman with the abusive husband finds a man who treats her so good that she overlooks the douche bag at home. The wife who put on 100 lbs. and refuses to go to the gym and doesn't care about looking good for her husband loses out to the hot chick at the gym who does care about how the husband views her body. External motivators can be independent or can build off internal motivators. Someone can give motivation by knowingly or unknowingly satisfying an external and/or internal need requirement. That is where, as the primary lover, it is your responsibility to do what you can to remove the internal motivation. There are enough external motivators without you giving more reason.

Catalyst- The catalyst is everything that ties into

infidelity's formation. This is the person who is able to sense your needs and satisfy your desires and are the untapped fantasies that you yearn to fulfill. The woman who approaches you while you are away on business. The man who comes to the house while your husband is at work. The timing, the place, the moment where you bump into your coworker and touch longer than intended. That last bottle of alcohol. Now all of these are contingent on the former two factors (motivation and risk). No matter how drunk you are you are probably not going to go tongue down the hot bartender because the risk is too great, but the catalyst is what sets everything in motion.

Time- All of these factors happen over a time period. Time does heal wounds, what counts is when the wound is treated. If you cut your hand and do nothing about it, eventually it grows worse and the infection spreads. When time is added to existing issues, like the motivation to cheat over a long time, infidelity will occur. PRESENT ISSUES LEFT UNATTENDED ONLY GET WORSE. Don't forget that.

Ex Factor- *The first time I cheated was spiteful and childish. Actually any form of cheating is spiteful and childish. However, I tried to justify my actions because of my motive. SHE gave me the reason. I blamed her for my immaturity. I was young, and in a relationship with the one I will call "the Tempest." The stories I could tell about her and her temper would be a book in its own right, but for this section we are focused on me.*

I was scheduled to participate in a national medical conference, she was taking a trip to go to her hometown, the same place where the love of her life resided. We were both going to be gone at the same time and she called me with some concerns. Her concern was that if she saw this guy it would awaken unresolved emotions and feelings she had for him. She said she owed it to herself to find out if she still cared for him. Without regard to our current relationship she made plans to see him. I asked her not to. She insisted she needed to and nothing I said would change her mind. She left on her trip, I went to my conference and I had all the items necessary to cheat (low risk, high motivation, and a catalyst who was willing).

So while away, I did it. I cheated and I felt no remorse for it. Had I left with the assumption that my lover was thinking of me instead of some other guy, maybe this wouldn't have happened. But there are no take-backs in the game of love. I came back from the conference and she said that seeing her ex did nothing. She hugged me happy to see her lover. We continued on as if nothing happened because as far as she knew, nothing did.

There are three instances where the formula does not apply.

1) *Sexual addiction-* I have actually had the displeasure of dating a REAL sex addict. (No ladies, your boyfriend who likes to have sex more than twice a day is not a sex addict). As much sex as I have had in my life, I thought that I was a sex addict. I was wrong. To put in perspective (and this is from the mouth of the addict I dated) it is the same urge that one who was addicted to drugs would feel. A compulsive need to have sex. There is no logic or reasoning involved in this process. For them, they have an itch and they will scratch it by any means necessary. The girl I dated wanted me to come home from work to have sex with her. I

have more sense than to throw away a job over sex, so she found someone else to take my place. She told me afterwards and there were no hard feelings. She explained her condition and I understood.

2) *They leave you* - This is when the person recognizes how dire their situation is. Either they care about you that much or they don't want to go down that road for their own sake. Either way, they feel leaving you is better than the alternative.

3) *They give up on you* -If the formula fails for this reason, then you have reached a point of no return. This is when your Lover has completely given up on you. They have been looking for an out and could careless if you find out. This is usually when a relationship has become a battlefield and the intention is to hurt you. I feel for anyone who goes through this.

Things to look for:

Changes in behavior- You and your lover used to talk all the time but now all you get is one word answers. They leave earlier or come home later from work. They call you less than before. Stopped saying, "I love you," on the phone. These changes need to happen multiple times before it can be considered a behavior change.

Not wanting to have sex- Whether it is the, "I'm too tired," excuse or just an overall aversion to sex, this is something to be mindful of. Lifestyle changes do have an effect on sexual desire, so be selective about when you note this as an issue. If your boyfriend took on a second job, he may genuinely be tired. If your wife is at home with your newborn, sex may not be on her mind.

Spending a lot of time on social media- Social media is an example of a catalyst that makes cheating easier. You can talk to people from around the world without anyone knowing about it. Social media is a double edged sword because if you suspect it and you are wrong, you have violated your lover's trust. Look for serious changes, like if your partner is waking up early or staying up late just to be on social media, or hiding/deleting messages

More time away from you- They are always finding excuses to get out the house and away from you. Ladies night, poker night, the gym. The fact is, they are really probably going to these places but the goal is to get away from you. Either you make them feel guilty or frustrate them with their decision to go out.

Changes in appearance- Your lover spends more time getting dressed or in the mirror. He shaves more closely. She wears makeup all the time now. Most people downplay their looks over time with one partner. If you notice that their appearance has become more important to them, it may not be caused by you but by a means to impress someone else.

Phone secrecy- Going into another room to talk on the phone. Texting and hiding their phone. Phone always on vibrate. These are things that should be signs of unfaithfulness.

Differences in Sex - If you are planning to cheat, the key to getting away with it is selecting the right catalyst, keeping it to yourself; and not connecting with your catalyst. The catalyst should be someone who accepts the role of being a side person and not care about getting promoted to anything more. No matter how much you trust your best friend or your sister or your boss, NEVER TELL ANYONE. Every time I was cheated on, the person who made me suspect what was going on was the friend, not the girl I was with. They may not say anything however, changes in behavior, discomfort in your presence, avoiding eye contact are some clear signs that somethings going on.

Insecurities- They constantly seem worried about you cheating and accuse you all the time of cheating or having someone on the side. That is because they think you are doing what they are. People who can't trust you (without reason) cannot be trusted.

If you have been cheated on, it is not the end. Deal with the "me issues" of relationships or the factors that you contributed to and I would advise asking a non-biased party their opinion. If you find some things you did contribute to the cheating, work on those things. Fix them and don't take them into the next relationship. If after some thought you determined it was not your actions that lead to the infidelity, then the only mistake is that you chose poorly. Your decision to date the cheater is still a choice you made. It is unfortunate that you chose someone you thought would love you and ended up hurting you. Now you know that it is not you as a person, but the incompatibility of you and someone else. Choose better next time. Don't dwell on what you could have done. Think instead of what you will do next time.

21

<u>Side Piece Survival</u>

<u>Guide</u>

<u>Ex Factor-</u> *Most women I had dealt with were not honest enough about the men they were dealing with. They would either lie and downplay their existence, or deny that they are even involved with someone. So I was a little bit caught off guard when I met 'the Hustler." A woman with an ebony complexion and the body of a video vixen. I was drawn to her purely for the sake of her resistance to my advances. I put in years of subtly making moves on her. She worked three jobs while being in school, so my ability to get time with her was limited. I was determined though, and would not be swayed from my goal. After* *a year had passed, I finally got her phone number and a shot at a date. I wasn't going to mess this up.*

Because I perceived this to be a one shot deal, I had to be very flexible and work with her schedule. That meant making myself available whenever she was ready. So when I got the call I told my friends to clear out and I made the proper arrangements. She came over, still dressed in her work attire-and she followed me upstairs to my apartment. I let her in, she asked if she could smoke which was a huge turn off for me but for this to happen I made the exception, so I let her. She looked at me calmly and said, "Before we go any further, I do want you to know, I like you, but I am seeing another guy and I've been seeing him for years now. Anything that happens with me and you won't change what I have going on with him. Are you okay with that?" I recognized instantly what she was asking me: Are you okay with being the guy on the side? Little did she know, for this to happen, I would have agreed to anything.

There are people who are perfectly content with casual encounters, especially those that come without the same obligations of a relationship. They have no qualms about being with someone else's lover and love to reap the rewards that come from the companionship that they give. They can easily be seen as the bad guy for not conforming to normal relationship standards. Get your own man, right? Why would you steal someone else's girl? However, everyone has their own individual wants and needs. These people focus on the wants and are usually indifferent to the consequences of their actions. If love is a game, they are the free agents, not loyal to any team, only loyal to their own interests. But they are only inches from calamity's caress. How do you bob-and-weave to dodge the punches that come from messing with someone's relationship? Everything you do should be geared towards survival.

Know your role- If you are the catalyst, the side piece, the other man or woman, then you have a role to play. Understanding your role and how important it is for you to STAY there is crucial to your romantic survival. You wouldn't take Cam Newton and make him play on the offensive line, that's not his role and he probably would not do very well . In the same sense, you should not step beyond the scope of what you are needed for. If what you are needed for is sex (not all side pieces are) then make that the focal point when you are present. If you are the "fun one," then don't ruin your time by trying to have discussions about a serious relationship. Playing in position gets you recognized as a constant in that person's life. As long as you don't make waves, you are in good standing. You are also likely to reap more benefits when you do NOT try to play another role.

   Be what the other isn't- There is something about you that your guy or girl likes. Whatever it is I can guarantee you that this trait or factor is not present, or is barely visible, in the person the initiator is currently with. It is side piece suicide for you to try and copy aspects of their relationship. In doing that you will drive them back to that person. (They are with you now because you possess something different, why be the same?) You also become a reminder, a guilt trip. He mentions that his wife always took him to a certain restaurant,what would possess you to go there as well? No, take this time to stand out. Create new memories. Every moment that they are with you should be memorable. They should be with their lover thinking of the next time they will see you. If you try to focus on getting what their primary lover has, you will ultimately fail and lose out on what you currently have.

Be selfless- Make them feel like they are the most important thing when they are with you. Be appreciative of EVERYTHING. He can only see you once a month, but when he does see you make it seem like you have waited all month for him. She calls only when he is at work, so give her the perception that you understand and are grateful just to hear her voice. Make it about them and in return they will be more inclined to make everything about you.

Never commit- Does this mean be single forever? No. But getting caught up in feelings that you can't build on is a mistake. You have set expectations and now you want more than you were promised. As the catalyst, realize that you are only filling a void for someone. Most times no matter what they say, they will always care more for their primary Lover. Stay in your role but prepare yourself for the day when they no longer need or want you. The thing about being the player on the bench is there is always a the potential to get called into the game. When you commit yourself and catch feelings, you make yourself vulnerable to someone who has NO OBLIGATION TO YOU. That is asking to get hurt. Instead, have fun with it while it lasts. Be grateful for the time and if it becomes more, great.

Don't make it personal- As long as you are in this role, you will never be first priority. Husbands and wives come first, kids come first, the family dog comes first. You are a filler for the initiator. Do not be offended by this. You are the dessert, not always needed, but always appreciated. You have value to them and that is important, so when you call and they hang up on the second ring don't take it personal. When they cancel last minute, don't take it personal. When they are too tired to be with you because being a wife or a husband or boyfriend or girlfriend has drained their energy, it is okay, don't *take it personal.*

Always be the best sex ever- It is POINTLESS for you to be the person they come to for sex and not make having sex with you an unforgettable experience. Now, I know everyone is not as talented as everyone else. There are physical components that play into a sexual experience, but intent and desire go a long way to creating an amazing romp in the bedroom. If you are the person on the side and you are lazy in bed, bad in bed, or withholding sex, you are asking to get cut off. Be a porn star for them. Your value will rise.

Be mobile and ready to go at all times- A quick way to get yourself dropped is to not be available when called upon. Though it is not fair, it is to be expected. You are an invader in something already established. You do not have rights. You cannot make demands. In order for what you have to "work," you must be available when called. An NFL team drafts a player out of college. They saw something in that player. They have a "relationship"with that player. But if that player doesn't come to practice they will get dropped from the team. Think of yourself as that player. Every time you are needed you have to be ready to suit up and come in the game. The more time you get in the game, the closer you get to a starting position.

Know when to cut ties- There may be times where you (for your own sake) have to be ready to exit stage left. You should never FIGHT for someone who already belongs to someone else. If you FIGHT you will be in a losing battle. Humbly know when to step back, know when to be silent, know when you need to disappear. You may be put in situations where you have to deny, lie or do other things in order to protect your position. Sometimes, you have to fall back in order to move forward.

Be their Number one fan- Most of the time you are going to have to deal with the issues that are not resolved by their current lover. My wife never supports me, my husband never takes me anywhere, etc. You must become their release. I used to thoroughly enjoy going to strip clubs. A lot of men who go there do not go there to see naked women. If all you want to do is look you can do that at home with an Internet connection and a bottle of lotion. No, they go because the women there are encouraged to stroke your ego. Even if they do it for the money, the men don't care because they need to hear that a woman needs them. They need to feel that desire those women create. If you are the side piece there should never be a moment where they doubt you want them. In the eyes of the initiator (the cheater) you are the good guy and their significant other is the bad guy. So keep appearing good by doing and saying all the right things. I support you, I care for you, I'm here for you.

Create a new world- One of the most important things you can do is BEthe escape. He or she will come to you in their time of need. They will come to you needing medicine that only you can give. They will come to you empty expecting you to fill them up. You will feel like you are being used. The truth is, you are, but you will be using them the same way. To fulfill your needs, whether physical, emotional, financial or other reasons, you are receiving a benefit from their presence just as they are from yours. It is not about fairness but about understanding your role and being grateful for what you are receiving.

Nothing lasts forever. If you want your position to change, patience and persistence is key. Just remember, if they stepped out to be with you, they can step out on you.

22

Sex Sex Sex, Now

What's Next?

Sex vs Making love - I'm going to put the age old debate to rest. Let us understand that the act of making love and sex are the EXACT SAME thing. They just have a different perspective when entering into the scenario. Just because he takes his time freaking, you doesn't mean he's "making love." Just because she's doing flips all over the bedroom doesn't mean she's not loving you. Before you create arguments in your mind saying "he's not talking about love making, that's just sex" I've said it here. They are the same. You can ask a guy who has absolutely no feelings for you to "make love" to you and he will, (I often did this because more women want to make love than have sex or any other vulgar term you can use to describe it). The type of sex you have does not indicate how they feel about you. During sex, the "Love Drug" is going to be released in the brain regardless causing the Pseudo-love effect.

Pseudo-love effect- The feelings experienced after sexual encounters that resemble love due to similar chemicals being released in the brain that are temporary and fade shortly after the encounter.

Everyone experiences this, unless the sex is unwanted. But in normal situations, there is a temporary fondness felt towards those we engage sexually that lasts for varying amounts of time depending on the person. For some the feeling lasts only minutes after. Others it can be days after where they still have romantic feelings founded on a sexual situation. The mistake comes when this pseudo-love is confused for true emotions and you make this the justification for a relationship. This is an argument that supports "not giving it up" on the first date. But that's just one side.

Ex Factor-*I was 18 years old, a freshmen in college without a care in the world. At this point my abilities in the bedroom were peaking. I had gained plenty of experience in the time leading up to my arrival at school. With every women I bedded I learned one lesson. That good sex had some very addictive properties. If you put it down just right, like a fiend, they will keep coming back for more. For most the experience was overwhelming. A kiss here, a touch there, and they were putty in my hands. The emotions that come from intimacy are so close to that of love, that a lot of women confused those feelings for being the authentic. I have fell into that trap before myself. But since I was usually the one initiating, I knew exactly what was going on.*

I had an insatiable sexual appetite. Some days, having as many as three different women in the same 24 hour period. Like breakfast lunch and dinner, I liked variety but I think I was still ultimately looking for someone who could quench my desire for pleasure. That is when I met "Lust" a chocolate woman with thick shapely proportions and a desire for sex that matched my

own. On the first night we experienced each other, and 12 more

times for the next 3 days. Before I knew it we had a regimen of

vigorous sex five times a day. We poured our all into every

moment, once running a record breaking eight hours love making

session. But when the school year ended so did our romp. As I

was not around to "satisfy" her thirst, she found another to stand

in my stead. In that time I had convinced myself this was love.

With the abundance of emotions flooding my system on a

continuous basis it had to be. Unbeknownst to me, I had become

addicted to that same drug that I had dealt to so many before.

When I was forced to go cold turkey, I did not fare so well.

Timing for sex-Women enjoy sex as much as men do.

Although it is said that's all we care about,sex is very important

for women and can easily be a deal-breaker So we all want it, but

who wants it more and when is the question. The exception of

waiting until marriage (a now foreign concept for most people) is

never agreed upon. Oh your boyfriend may "agree" to wait until

your ready when the truth was that he wanted to have sex three weeks ago. First piece of information that you must accept is that someone's approach to you in regards to sex comes from your presentation. Just as a lion does not approach an animal he doesn't believe be can take down. People don't present sex to their lover unless given the perception that they can get it. This rule goes for both men and women alike, however it rings true more so for men approaching women. So if you feel like guys only approach you for sex you need to reassess your love brand and what it says about you. Some people suggest waiting 90 days to have sex. I am 100% against any type of time restriction on sex and here is why.

1) *It starts the relationship with a promise of sex-* When you tell your lover that you wait "X" number of days before having sex, it makes a promise of intimacy that you may not keep. For one, you better make sure your personality is amazing if you're going to be withholding sex. Because lack of sex will not make a man or woman stay faithful to you. But now you have created an expectation of reward that may be undeserved.

2) *It creates a scenario where sex is a bargaining tool-*

You have begun whatever relationship you have on the premise that you control sex. This is true, however, your sex shouldn't be something you lock away and pull out only when you're ready. Many relationships fail because the woman attempts to leverage sex as some type of bargaining chip. "I won't give you any if you don't do what I want" This is the fast track to getting replaced or getting cheated on.

3) *If the sex is bad (deal-breaker bad)*- Nothing is worse than waiting all that time, building up all the anticipation for sex that is, in a word, awful. Sometimes you can work on sex together, but at such an early point in your relationship, have you determined that person is worth the investment? If not you've wasted that many months of your time. From my experience with women (Which is more extensive than most people) *most* women are not as good at sex as they *think* they are. Taking a chance on unknown sex is like getting promised candy and hoping you don't end up with something sugar free.

4) *There is no guarantee that you will know this person any better in that time period*. What amount of time is right? At

what point do you truly know someone? I can tell you that even after six months of dating you'll still be finding out things about your lover that you didn't know before. Truth is there is NO FORMULA for when is the "right time". People are complex, so how do you know that going out every weekend for three months straight will uncover all you need to feel comfortable enough to have sex. The answer is you don't.

5) *It creates an endpoint*- You unknowingly create the deadline for your own relationship. If you are not on-point then you can potentially set the timeline for someone else to exit. If things are going "so so" that individual can easily wait until they get "the goods." Instead I encourage you to have a mature conversation about your wants needs and expectations in regards to romance. Once you've had that conversation make a mental checklist with the criteria that you want met before YOU are ready for sex. For example: I need to know he respects me, I need to know he isn't sleeping with other women, I need to know what his goals are. I need to know it's safe to have sex with him. Once you have established that all of these things checkout why

wouldn't you enjoy the physical aspects of love. Everyone's
checklist will be different based on what's important to you.

90 days doesn't mean you're ready, Guy or girl. You could
be ready for sex in 20 days but would continue to wait 70 because
of a rule. Not all men (or women) are willing to wait for sex. You
could miss out on someone making you happy over a "rule "
There are people I know who combine finances before they
combine bodies. That is backwards. Sex is important but it is
NOT the defining moment of relationships.

Sex and psychology- Sex itself has its own personality, its
own identity that is unique to the person you're sleeping with.
These traits are built around that persons psychology and
eventually comes out during intercourse. Understand that a person
shows you who they truly are during sex. That is the moment
when we are most honest. We can't hide who we are. We can hide
motives and facts but the essence of who we are comes out in the
bedroom. This is a fact I myself didn't realize until later in
adulthood. Think about it. Selfish people have selfish sex. Giving
people have generous or selfless sex. Is sex the basis for getting to

completely know someone? Absolutely not. However when. You become intimate with someone there are certain truths about a person's character that they cannot hide during sex. Pay attention

Good and Bad sex, Plus how to be better- You've heard me refer to sex as a sport before. Not just because it's requires two seemingly opposing forces engaged in physical activity. Like any sport there are rules and different roles positions and levels. EVERYONE IS NOT GOOD AT SEX. Some can coach and can't play. Some are bench warmers, some are all stars and some are cheerleaders. Good sex is a great thing. So how do you know that your sex is good? There are really only two sure ways to know. Your sex is good if one, the people that you have sex with tell everyone how good it is. Or two when taking away your sex is not an option. People let you know when your sex is good but do not let you know when it's bad. So I'm gonna give you some tips on how to improve your performance.

1) *Change your perception*- As we think so we are. Perceptions about sex can be limiting or liberating depending on our stance. When you view certain things in sex negatively, your

subconscious brings those views forward in performance. Sometimes all that is needed is an attitude adjustment. Look at things from a new angle and your sex will follow suit.

2) *Change your approach*- Every encounter is situational. Sometimes you have to take the lead. Sometimes you have to ride shotgun. Being oblivious to the mood, rhythm, or desires of your lover because you already had a preconceived idea of what you were going to do is a quick way to get labeled as a bad lover. Discuss the things that your lover likes. Make an effort to understand the mood and match your rhythm with theirs. If you have no rhythm, let someone else drive.

3) *Be open to criticism* - A closed minded lover is a bad lover. This doesn't mean you have to be willing to do things that are beyond your level of freaky. What it means though is that when your lover tells you how you can be better *for them* you don't completely shut then down. Sometimes it's not that you're doing it wrong, it's that your doing it different from the way they like. Be willing to adjust, be flexible in the bedroom, and I promise even your willingness to bend for your lover will raise

your value in their eyes.

4) *DO something different*- When you do the same thing ALL the time it can get boring. You must work to keep a certain level of spontaneity in your sex life. Don't be afraid to try new positions, new places, even sex at a different time of day. (Studies show most women prefer early morning sex. Rise and shine buddy). Any type of variation keeps you from being labeled as a boring sexual partner. Do it on the couch instead of the bed. Start in the car, in the kitchen. Make sex fun and enjoy yourself. If you see it as a job, you'll treat it the same way. Remember you want your sex to be a memorable experience. Not something that someone would want to forget.

5) *Practice*- Everything gets better with practice. It's hard to practice without a regular partner, however, that alone time is when you need to reflect on how you perform and how to improve. If you become disheartened about sex you'll never get better. Keep at it slugger. You'll get there.

Sex is a major milestone in all relationships but after that it's the maintenance that's important. Staying on top of your game, not getting lazy, and making it enjoyable is how you will keep

yourself and your lover satisfied.

23

<u>Lover's Evolution</u>

Who is the love of your life? Is it the guy you dated back in high school? Is it your college sweetheart? Or maybe it is the girl who showed you how to love? Could it be the first person you were intimate with? Maybe the love of your life is your spouse? If you answered anywhere in this ball park then I will tell you that your love has been misplaced.

The key to having successful relationships begins with having a strong core. That core is self-love. It fuels everything that you do in relationships. You must appreciate YOU. You must like YOU. You must be ok with spending time with just YOU. In early chapters we discussed how it was important to KNOW who you are. But knowing is not enough. Self-hate is the cornerstone for destructive relationships. Look at yourself in the mirror and fall in love with the person you are.

We often get bogged down focusing on our own flaws. Guess what? You have to love those too. They are only flaws because we classify them that way. We place too much importance on being seen as normal. The only normalcy is to be abnormal. People are not built on a conveyor belt and spit out for the world to see. We are products of different systems. We developed as we were meant to. Since this is true, that means you developed perfectly to your design. Don't worry about everyone else. You are perfect as you are.

Spend time loving yourself. The more you love you, the more others will be drawn to you. You receive love like a bucket getting water poured in. You are meant to fill up as you are loved. However if you don't love yourself, your bucket has a hole in it. Fill that with love for self.

So why should you love you? Because you deserve to be loved. Because the most important person in your life is you.

Because no one should have the ability to lower your self worth. Because you are meant to love and be loved. We don't need to find someone to complete us. We need to seek to be whole and then seek love. So love yourself. You're worth it.

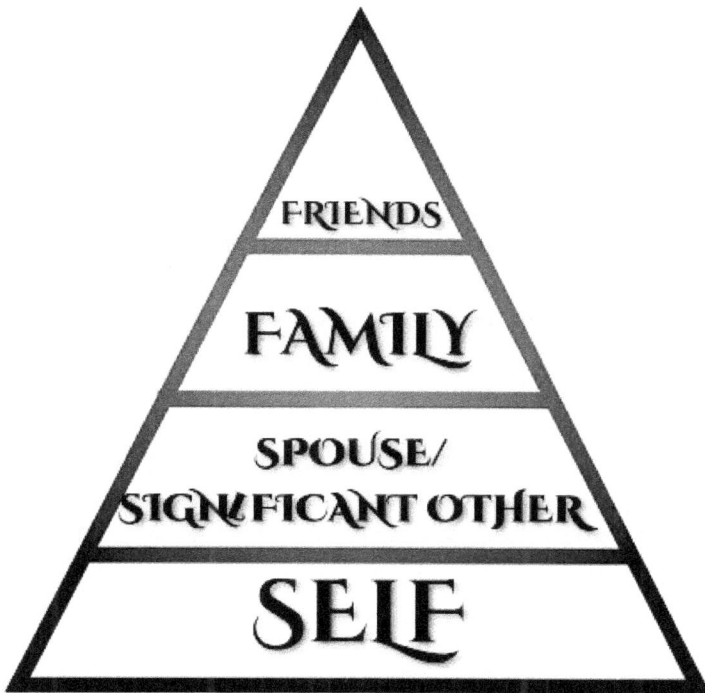

The Lover that we were before does not have to be what remains. The experiences we go through have the ability to shape us for the better if we allow them. Our resistance to change is really just a refusal to better ourselves. A defiant stance against our own happiness. We often become unhappy because of the actions of someone else. Who gave them the key to your joy? You did. So take it back and take control of how YOU feel about you. We have to be more. If you take anything at all from The Lover's Man-ual, it's that you have a responsibility to make the changes necessary to bring you romantic happiness. So what's stopping you.

Stressors- Evolution does not spontaneously occur. It is not magic so for it to occur in a relationship, something has to prompt a change in you. For me, it took continuous heartbreak and an abundance of relationship let downs. It took me getting tired of always running and never having something of value. It took me almost completely giving up on love for me to see that I needed to change.

In evolution, it is believed that some stimuli must be present in order to initiate evolution. That is to say a bird wouldn't develop green feathers unless for its survival it became necessary to do so. So in the same sense you have to recognize a need to evolve in your relationships. Are you crying all the time because of emotional neglect. Then it's necessary to make the changes necessary to survive in your relationship. Are you constantly *spending* money on someone in your relationships? Do you always feel sexually empty? These are things that should trigger a response from you. That response should be to make your love life evolve into one that ensures your loves survival. This may mean dating someone new. It may mean making changes in your perception of relationships. It could even mean making changes to yourself. But whatever it is make the change.

Apex- I spoke briefly before about what it meant to be an apex predator. Nothing preys on you, EVER. So now we take the tools that we have been given and the lessons we have learned and we build our arsenal. We fortify our hearts against any potential invaders that are not here for our benefit and stand strong, with confidence in the new lover we have become. You must put into practice the lessons you've learned and become the victor in love, instead of the victim. Do not engage in romantic activities that you know are contrary to your love. A tiger is an apex predator in its environment. So a tiger would not decide to go deep sea fishing in the middle of the ocean. If it did it would be knocked off the top of its food chain. Recognize when certain people or behaviors have the potential to throw you off your game and avoid them like the plague. Establish yourself as the ruler of your fate and NEVER let anyone take that from you

Love evolved- When you look back at how you loved and were loved before, you should see a tremendous difference. You'll see less excuses and more execution as you make the decisions that benefit your life and your love as a whole. You'll begin to recognize the traps others may set for you and be able to maneuver through relationships without constantly falling into peril. You will have confidence in your ability to love someone else, by knowing the differences in styles of love and methods of receiving love. Your ex will look at you (probably wishing they were still with you) and realize that you're not the same person they had been with before. But most of all, you can take love, and from this point forward know that you are getting the most out of it, instead of it getting the most out of you. It's time to let your love evolve. Look to your future with the faith, that you can offer yourself and someone else a healthy Love life and that you don't have to be mastered by it anymore.

NEXT Factor- *I was 26 years old and I had all but given up on relationships. I had been beaten down by love again and again, coming up short time after time. I no longer believed that "the one" existed. I had convinced myself that based on statistics, everyone wasn't going to find someone. I was done chasing fairly tales. I decided, instead, to focus on internal happiness. I would be spending time getting to know, love, and forgive myself for the person I had been before. It was time to heal.*

I will call her "My Angel." Truly in my suffering there was some divine intervention on my love life. There was was a sense of fate in our meeting. We had been around each other many times, and yet I had never noticed her presence. Even at our first introduction, I barely paid any attention to her. At that time, she was with someone else so she probably registered as "off limits" for me. It wasn't until her relationship ended and we had a casual conversation about matters unrelated that I noticed it. She was different.

We exchanged numbers, and our first phone conversation lasted hours from the night until the the early morning hours. This may seem like nothing to most people, but for someone like me who hates to be on the phone, it was a milestone. She had depth, she was intelligent, she was creative and adventurous. She was all that and more. I checked mental attraction off my list, even going as far as to tell her that I would make her mine during that first conversation. I'm sure she thought I was nuts but I knew, she just had to be convinced.

We set our first "date," watching movies together at my place. Movies are big for me, and I needed to know that we could connect in more ways than just on the phone. As she pulled up to the house, I waited outside and watched her approach. I vaguely remembered her physical appearance from our first introduction. But when she approached me now, I could not help but thank God for the "angel" he had sent to me. Skin like cinnamon, full lips and eyes of wonder. She was perfection. Her body was like that of a work of art. Just the sight of her made my more primal instincts bubble to the surface. I wanted her. Physical attraction...check.

Now I was in a rough place in my life at this point in time. As I was in a process of rebuilding myself. I should have been walking around with an "under construction" sign hanging from my neck Financially I was struggling. I had a vehicle that broke down every other week. Part of the reason I wasn't dating when I met "My Angel" was because of car trouble. It's hard to be a good lover when you can't go anywhere or afford to pay for anything. So when I broke down on the side of the road and she offered not only to give me a ride home but to take me to work the next day I was 100% sure she was "The One." Which is why after only a few weeks of dating I asked her to marry me. I know that sounds insane. But that was 3 years ago and in 4 months she will be changing her name to mine and becoming my wife. I cannot explain the totality of the emotion I feel when I am around her. I AM better when I'm with her. She is the woman I had been waiting for. I redefined love when I looked at her. I would have gladly had a million bad relationships if I knew the end result would have still been her. It took me going through the trial and error, mishaps and mistakes, experiencing loss and learning loves

lessons in order for me to finally reach a point where I was

capable of providing and receiving the best love possible. I owe it

to her. To myself. To be the best lover possible. Now, for the rest

of my life, that's what I'm going to be.

Sources Cited

1. Lumpkin, Sydney. "Can Facebook Ruin Your Marriage?."

ABC News. ABC News. Web. n.d. 24 May 2012

http://abcnews.go.com/technology/facebook-relationship-

status/story?id=16406245

www.ingramcontent.com/pod-product-compliance
Lightning Source LLC
Chambersburg PA
CBHW060010050426
42448CB00012B/2692